The Good Son

What our Father in Heaven expects of us

Dr Timothy Sng

The Good Son - What our Father in Heaven expects of us
Publisher: Dr Timothy Sng with Amazon
Copyright 29.7.2018 Dr Timothy Sng

ISBN 978-967-16824-1-8

Amazons Edition, License Notes & Acknowledgments

ACKNOWLEDGMENT

All thanksgiving and praise go to our Heavenly Father, THE LORD GOD ALMIGHTY and to Jesus, the Good Son, and the Holy Spirit of God, our Counsellor.

I deeply appreciate my family, commencing with my beloved wife Jane, children Grace & husband David, son John & wife Vicky, and son Chris & wife Grace for their love, support, prayers and suggestions and input.

I am particularly grateful for Pastor Reuben Seevaratnam, author of "Generational Alignment' for his review, suggestions and comments.

Sincere appreciation to my teachers, mentors, friends and fellow itinerant ministers who have journeyed with me through nearly four decades in the faith, many of whom have written commendations here.

Special thanks go to many who spend time having fellowship one-to-one and face-to-face or on the phone, even across the globe, clocking hundreds and hundreds of hours. These direct or 'phone fellowship', some simple chats, good fellowship, some counselling, often with prayers - sometimes daily, often weekly, for a season, with each chat going on for anything from a few minutes to a good full hour have been a great source of strength to me. They have been energizing, good Godly advice, effective counsel, often ministering to the soul, and consolidated with prayers, which sooth and heal the soul.

Their first names are as follows: "Thanks dear friends, from Tek Seng, Tuan Soon, Peter Tong (departed), Sam Abraham (departed), Siok Beng, Crystal (Pastor), John Williams (Pastor), Esther, Elsie, Mercy, Grace, Meyria, Gary, Poh Choong, Ezekiel (Bishop), Samy Davies (departed) and Jesudason (Pastor) for input and investing in my life and walk with the LORD."

I personally thank pastors, teachers, mentors, ministers, prophets, speakers, preachers, visitors from near and far who have ministered to me through close one-to-one ministry, direct prayers and personal prophecies, counselling and powerful rhema words and teachings during their friendship, or at their conferences, that have contributed immensely to my personal walk and growth over the years.

Mentors and ministers include Pastor Dr Chew Weng Chee, and others (Pastors and lay ministers) James Santhosam (Bishop), Brother See Lok, Paul Ang, Stanley Lim, Joseph Selva & Lily, George Theva (all Pastors) and Ezekiel (Bishop).

Finally, thanks to all my personal pastors & shepherds, beginning with the Good Shepherd Himself, and in chronological order Pastors John Watterson, Winston Edip, Osh Ong, George Pledger, Tony Tan, Michael Song, Kelly & Suen Yap and Pastor Dr Chew Weng Chee & Pastor Dr Lee Choo (since 2003 till the present) for their teaching, guidance, nurturing, prayers, support and friendship, while under their able and loving pastoral care and watchful eyes.

I appreciate being enriched by the countless Christian authors, reading wonderful biographies, listening to dozens of famous conference speakers, and many Christian leaders on audio and U-tube.

Thank you, Father God, Jesus, my Lord & Savior, and the Holy Spirit our Counsellor, who dwells in me, and is a part of my thought life, ministering to me always through the Word, many teachers, and directly to my inner man, through dreams, visions, and the still small, soft and audible voice.

2 Corinthians 6:18

*"I will be a Father
To you,
And you shall be My sons
And daughters,
Says
The LORD Almighty."*

The Good Son

What our Father in Heaven expects of us

Dr Timothy Sng

SYNOPSIS

What does our Father in Heaven expect of us as a son or daughter? What would our role and responsibility be as a son or daughter of God? We often hear the quote from William Ernest Henley, expressed personally: "I am the master of my fate and the captain of my soul". Not necessarily so, when we have a Father in Heaven. While it is true that the LORD

GOD, our Father in Heaven has given man & woman a lot of liberty and freedom, and also a very strong mandate to 'multiply, fill the earth, rule and have dominion over it', we do have a duty to the LORD. This duty can be summed up in one word, - 'LOVE', i.e. to love God with all our heart, all our might, all our mind and all our soul.

Meditating on the above question, "What does our Father in Heaven expect of us?", Timothy Sng comes out with a list of a dozen things to remind us what we should and can do to please our Father. This list differs from the Ten Commandments, because it is more than that and beyond for the 'son'. The son is no longer under the law, but surpasses it to a new and higher level of intimacy with our Father in Heaven. When our relationship with our Father in Heaven is set right, and we draw close to Him, arriving at a new level of intimacy with our Father, it will be a fulfilling life of abundance and success, all for God's Glory. The first important step towards pleasing God is to acknowledge Him, and call upon His Name: 'THE LORD'.

CONTENT

FOREWORD

Commendations & Testimonies about Author

Departing from the norm of writing a review of the book "The Good Son", this author humbly requested friends and ministers to write 'just a few lines' of testimonies for the author, being an unknown Christian author from Kuala Lumpur, Malaysia. Even though some dozen plus e-books on faith have been in circulation for a decade now, the name 'Timothy Sng' is still new.

I have known Dr Timothy Sng for well over fifteen years now as his Senior Pastor, as a fellow medical colleague, but more importantly as a friend. I frequently pray for him in my devotions, and cover his beloved family in my prayers throughout all these years.

Over the years I have seen him grow strong, resolute in his faith and in his love for Jesus. He has served faithfully in his cell, in missions to poorer countries and in speaking at many smaller churches to encourage them. It is in this area of encouragement that Dr Sng exercises his greatest gift. He is an encourager par excellence. He always has a positive word of encouragement to widows, single parents, the hurting, the grieving and the marginalized. Truly, as a born-again son of God, he bears the semblance of the Son of God.

I have the greatest respect and admiration for Dr Sng, who has been a great encouragement to me personally as well. I wish for him and his loved ones all the best that Almighty God can give.

Pastor Dr Chew Weng Chee
Senior Pastor & Founder, SIBKL (Sidang Injil Borneo, Kuala Lumpur)
Formerly Practicing Obstetrician & Gynecologist
(Currently, the author's Senior Pastor)

I know this man, Dr Timothy Sng – a man who does not let the left hand know what the right hand does. Dr Timothy Sng is like a man whom we read in the Bible, like David, who was a man after the heart of God. I would say with all humility that Dr Timothy Sng is a true man after the heart of God.

He is a man who always sets priority first to the lost souls, and secondly to those who have back-slided. Lastly, he has got a heart of carrying the Good News of Jesus Christ to the ends of the world. He will do it himself and he will also support other men and women of God to spread the Good News all over the globe.

My wife, Pastor Lily will say, "Dr Timothy Sng is a man of his words, and when he gives a word that he will give or support, he will not rest till he completes it.

Pastors Joseph & Lily Selva & Gloria Selva
Itinerant Ministers and Evangelists, Klang, Malaysia
(Pastor Joseph opened the door to ministry for the author, with his introduction and invitation to the first Full Gospel Businessman's Fellowship)

The good son is epitomized in Dr Timothy Sng's life, and daily walk with his heavenly father. Since coming to know God in a personal relationship, Timothy has consistently strived to live his life and walk in a way as a good son to bring glory to his Father.

Pastor Tony Tan,
Chairman/advisor,
Creation Community International AG, Malaysia.
(Author's former Pastor at Lifeline AOG Church, Kuala Terengganu, Malaysia,1982-1988)

Dr Timothy Sng is a very down to earth, passionate one-to-one evangelist, who seizes the 'Kairos' moments, when a soul crosses his path. His Christ-like gentle, helpful, considerate character and wisdom is a 'magnet', drawing and touching many who are searching for the truth. We pray that

God will use this humble servant of His to revolutionize and motivate many disciples to win more souls for His Glory and Honor. If everyone of us, lives our lives like Timothy to win souls, the whole earth will reverberate with His glory, in the years to come.

Pastor David Liew Chee Kien
Pastor (English Section) Saving Grace Church,
Kepong, Kuala Lumpur, Malaysia

I have known Dr Timothy Sng since 2005. He is a generous tent-maker, and supporter of smaller churches like GISM (Gereja Injil Sepenuh Malacca). Since I have known him, Dr Sng has never denied any requests for urgent needs or support. His deep concern for the church of Christ, servants of the LORD, his humility and ever ready assistance has been a tremendous encouragement to me and my service to God. We deeply appreciate and value his help and contributions, with gratitude, and wish him all the best in this endeavor as an author of "The Good Son". May God bless Dr Sng with manifold blessings for all his good work and generosity.

Pastor Vincent Tharuman Maniam
Senior Pastor, Gereja Injil Sepenuh, Sri Aman, Sarawak
(Translated: Full Gospel Church, Sarawak, formerly Senior Pastor GIS, Malacca)

I consider Dr Timothy truly a part of our family and a committed member of my church and ministry, Gereja Pentecosta Di Indonesia (The Pentecostal Church of Indonesia), Bukit Kemuning Branch, Shah Alam, Malaysia. Since 2014, he has ministered to us from the pulpit for over 30 Sundays, and was our camp speaker for the year 2015. He ministers in fluent Bahasa Indonesia, and speaks passionately for Jesus, from the Heart of God, through his heart to the congregation. He enjoys singing Batak hymns with the congregation.

His support for our ministry to the diaspora from Indonesia, and my family is deeply appreciated. We are blessed to know this man of God.
Pastor Joel Siregar
Senior Pastor, GPdI Bukit Kemuning, Shah Alam, Malaysia

I have known Dr Timothy Sng since our Primary school days. Dr Tim has a heart of compassion for people in general. He is a loving and caring person. He is also an evangelist at heart, and no matter what the situation he is in, he avails himself to boldly wins souls for our Lord.
Pastor Raymond Teoh
Pastor and Administrator, River of Life Sanctuary, Desa Sri Hartamas, Kuala Lumpur, Malaysia

Dr Timothy is a dedicated neurologist, a faithful husband to one wife, a loving father of three children and a good friend for many, both in his home land and around the globe. More than anything, he is a true 'lover of God.'
He was introduced to me not as a doctor, but as a 'friend of God' and there began our friendship more than a decade ago. I find that his zeal for God is vibrant, his love for God is unconditional, his faith in Him is ever increasing and his heart for the ministry and the ministers of God is ever expanding. He is one who keeps himself ready to speak for God in and out of season. He knows that "He who began a good work in him, will be faithful to complete it." Therefore, I find that nothing can stop him from running his race of life as he continues his good fight of faith for God.
Reverend Edward Francis
Senior Pastor, Bread of Life Church, Manipal, India.

I had the privilege to know Dr Timothy Sng from 1989, when he visited me in New Delhi, and again on my trips to Malaysia. I know he is a child of GOD, a man of GOD, and a bible student, as well as teacher with a passion to walk the talk first. I'm very impressed with his new book. It is birthed after spending long hours for many seasons of being in his own quiet prayer chamber with the Bible. The illumination he received from the Lord and reflected in this book is worth to chew and practice for any who desire to be a true disciple of the Lord and victorious Christian in his or her life, and working place. I strongly recommend this book to all who have a passion to grow in Christ.

dr p.g.vargis
founder and chief mentor, Indian Evangelical Team, India
(Author: IET has planted over 9000 churches, mainly in North India)

Dr Timothy Sng has been friends of Prince of Peace Ministry, India, and personal friends of me and my family for two decades. Apart from coordinating meetings and having fellowship during my ministry trips to Malaysia, he has visited Prince of Prince head church, several village churches and our prayer mountain, ministering to the flock wherever he went. His support, encouragement, prayers and commitment for Prince of Peace Ministries over two decades is deeply appreciated. As a co-laborer for the Kingdom of God, I thank God for his heart and passion. He is indeed an exemplary Marketplace minister and I commend Dr Tim's work as author of 'The Good Son' to you.

Bishop BA Santhosam
Founder & Bishop, Prince of Peace, India
(Prince of Peace India has over 350 village churches in South India)

I have known Dr Sng for a good number of years now. He has a tremendous heart for God and His Kingdom. God uses him greatly to advance the gospel by sharing the Word in the market places and also supporting financially many ministries and ministers.

Dr Sng has great passion too for mission and missionaries. God anoints him for understanding the Word and also receiving revelation from God. A man of integrity and one who walks in the fear of God, his book reflects his choice and desire for intimacy with God. I strongly recommend it for the works of ministry. He truly is God ordained for such a time as we approach the coming and arrival of our Lord Jesus Christ.

Timothy indeed is a true friend and a co-laborer in the Kingdom of God.

Pastor George G.A.Thevarakam
Itinerant Minister, Kingdom Faith Fellowship
International

Dr Timothy Sng is a man passionate for the Lord, seen in his passion for the lost. Besides always looking for opportunities to share the Good News of the Gospel to those who have not heard, he has other outstanding qualities of patience, generosity and the honor he demonstrates toward spiritual fathers and mothers of the faith, in seeking their advice and counsel. I am blessed and impacted by his diligent seeking, to know the heart of ABBA Father as a good son.

Pastor Reuben Seevaratnam
Lead Minister of Global Harvest Assembly, Penang,
Malaysia
Author of 'Generational Alignment'

To me, Dr Sng is a very passionate evangelist, more so than a doctor. I truly thank God for his passion for the lost. He may not be muscular or well built, but he is definitely a strong man of faith, as he speaks boldly, yet always filled with love. He remembers his patients, and cares for each one for their salvation. Despite many challenges and persecution, he continues to advance and overcome them, doing his best as the Lord leads him. I thank God for this life, in Timothy Sng.

Pastor Thomas Ling,
Pastor, Hope Church, Puchong, Kuala Lumpur.

Dr Tim is a man after God's very own heart. Despite his busy schedules he always finds time to share the Gospel, at every opportunity, so that many can come to know and receive Christ as their Lord and Savior."

Evangelist & Tentmaker Philip Ong
Go Forth Asia Board member, FGB Sunway Chapter President, and Gideons Petaling Jaya Camp President, Malaysia

Sng was the acting State Physician in Sarawak in the 1980s, when we witnessed the outpouring of the Holy Spirit in the churches. I have never ceased to marvel at his passion and zeal for evangelism. He has been used mightily in this area, and it will continue for His glory till He comes.

Dr Thomas Chung
Itinerant Preacher & Teacher of The WORD, Sarawak, Malaysia

It is my joy to commend Dr Timothy Sng to you. We were classmates in school in Kluang, Johor from 1958 to 1962, and reconnected only recently. I admire Dr Sng for his integration of Christian life with his professional life. He lives out a lifestyle of witness and testimony in church and ministry. He is also well known professionally with patients

coming from many countries. Matthew 5:16 best reflects his life: as doctor, writer, evangelist, friend, and preacher.
Reverend Dr M G George
Pastor of Malaysia Discipleship Center churches (1968-2016).
Currently, Pastor, Johor Bahru Disciples Church, Malaysia

I come across Dr Sng as someone that is passionate in sharing the gospel. He has no airs, though he is well qualified neurologist. Affable and friendly to all, he is kind and compassionate. For example, on my recent trip to Pantai Hospital to visit my sister, I bumped into Dr Sng, and he immediately accompanied me to see my sister, even though he was busy. He fervently prayed along with me. Such is his hospitality, helpfulness and ever willingness to minister to the sick. Indeed, my sister recovered soon after that. Praise the Lord!
Elder Dr Philip Chieng
Chairman & Elder, Praise Baptist Center, Board Chairman, World Outreach International, Malaysia

We have known Dr Timothy Sng personally for more than ten years. Not only is he an outstanding neurologist, but he really is a man after God's heart. Always ready to testify to God's love through his own experiences, Dr Sng is a fine example of one who not only preaches the Word but one who lives the Word.

We warmly recommend him and his writings which are a blessing to those who will have open hearts.
Reverend Steve Chang & Lily Chang
Senior Pastor, River of Life Sanctuary
Desa Sri Hartamas, Kuala Lumpur

In my opinion, Dr S'ng is a person who has a great burden for lost souls, with a deep agape love for those dear to him. For many years, I have witnessed the price he has paid for the salvation of some of these precious loved ones. Often, in order for Jesus to be glorified, he persevered and endured, looking up to the love of the Heavenly Father and the mercy of Jesus Christ. By the power granted to him by the Holy Spirit, Dr S'ng has been able to hold on to the present, and still not give up.

He is steadfast in his conviction of God's promises, and he tries his best to satisfy the Father's expectations of him. He believes that the difficulties and trials he has experienced has given him patience and a strong mind, and thus continues to run along the narrow path for the glory of the Father and the exaltation of the Lord Jesus Christ!

Reverend (Ms) Crystal Cheang
Crystalsea Prophetic Ministry, Author of "Wonderful Trip to Heaven"
Itinerant Minister, Dream Center, Ipoh, Malaysia

It has been a pleasure knowing Dr Timothy Sng over 14 years now. He is a wonderful doctor, and a great friend to all our family members. He models how we can face challenges with confidence and faith and he willingly communicates valuable lessons from his life experiences. This book is for all who desires to live out a well transformed life, drawing close to the Father.

Pastor (Ms) Inky Ong
Senior Pastor SIBKLCC, (Chinese Church) Kuala Lumpur

Brother Sng Kim Hock (Timothy) is passionate in reaching out to many in the market place fulfilling the Great

Commission. He is a great encourager who ministers in the power of the Holy Spirit. A humble servant of God, a prayerful son, full of grace and compassion like his Master.
Elder Ng Soon Gan
Elder & Past Chairman, Full Gospel Assembly, Kuala Lumpur

I have the pleasure of knowing Dr Sng for a number of years now and would like to take this opportunity to congratulate him on the publishing of his book 'The Good Son'. Dr Sng is an effective evangelist, as he has led more than 500 people to Christ! He is also a respectable preacher, who has preached over 130 messages in English, Bahasa Malaysia and Bahasa Indonesia. He is active sharing God's word in Klang Valley churches and Full Gospel Businessmen Chapters, and has been a speaker at several church camps. He prays over the sick regularly, and has seen miraculous recovery from critical illnesses, over the sick. Dr Sng's mission has covered trips to India, Indonesia, and the Middle East. Evangelism and leading people to Christ is in his 'heart beat'. May God continue to use him mightily in His Kingdom and for His glory! God's blessings on this servant's work and book: "The Good Son."
Reverend Dr K. James Solamadan
Retired Methodist Pastor, former Chairman of Methodist Tamil Council

I have known Dr Sng for more than 20 years. He has a tremendous heart for God and His Kingdom. God uses him greatly to advance the gospel by preaching the Word in the market places and also supporting (with his co-laborers) financially many ministries. Dr Sng has great passion too for both mission and missionaries. God anoints him for understanding the Word and also receiving revelation from God.

He seeks fervently after prophetic gifting and teaching, attending many seminars by apostles, prophets and teachers from all over the world, that come from USA, UK, India to bless many people in the region. As a man of integrity, he walks in the fear of God. I highly recommend him for ministry.

Dr Paul Ang
Founder Paul Ang Global Vision Ministry, former Pastor, Tabernacle of Glory, Kuala Lumpur, Malaysia

I met Dr Sng in 1997, by divine appointment. We were led to prayer, and I received a Word from the LORD for him. He was moved by the Holy Spirit and felt an awakening in his spirit and soul. Since then, I have witnessed his work and ministry increase and grow. Watching him over the years, I testify that he has been faithful in his walk with God, humble in his spirit, thirsty in his soul as he seeks after God, and runs after many men & women of God for prayers, anointing and teaching. He is a devout Christian doctor, neurologist and a living epistle to those who come across his life. His love for the LORD and the Word is evident, as I see him being 'sold out' for the Master, choosing to please Him always.
I have witnessed patients entering his clinic and coming out with a smile, as his speech and action speaks grace, love and compassion. Dr Sng is a generous Christian who gives his time, heart and freely to ministers in need.
May the Spirit of wisdom be upon him, as he writes from his heart.

Ms Grace Davies
Prophetic Ministry, Author of "Wilderness to Oasis"

Dr Timothy is a very close friend of my father, the Late Reverend Dr P.N.Samy Davis, Founder of Jesus Loves Ministries, with 18 branch churches in Malaysia. Dr Timothy himself has led over 500 souls to Christ, through direct

personal evangelism, especially in the marketplace. Dr Timothy preaches the Word of God in a very inspiring and encouraging way. The move of the Holy Spirit is evident in his ministry. A man full of God's love, he shows patience, demonstrates love through his deeds, supporting the ministry of God in many ways. May God bless his work exceedingly.
Reverend (Ms) Malina Davis Alfred
Co-President, Jesus Loves Ministries, Malaysia

As Dr Tim Sng's former Pastor in SIB Iris Garden, Kuching, Sarawak, it gives me great joy to know how the Lord has used him in the last 20 over years. I have known Tim to be a compassionate man with a passion for the lost. The angels in heaven rejoice in each person he led to know Jesus through this, His humble servant.

The Lord has given Tim the gift of an evangelist, confirmed in his effective ministry of bringing so many to the saving knowledge of Jesus. I look forward to reading "The Good Son", and to be inspired by another servant of the Lord.
Reverend Osh Ong
Former Senior Pastor, Chinese Church, London &
Ambassador of Tearfund, Evangelical Alliance, Global
Connections & COCM, United Kingdom
(Author's former Pastor, SIB Iris Garden, Kuching, Sarawak, Malaysia)

" Call upon Me and I will answer you " Jeremiah 33:3
Father God heard me and sent His messenger Dr Timothy Sng Kim Hock, Consultant Neurologist.

In my distress, Timothy Sng flew into Singapore from Kuala Lumpur, and spent time on my side, praying and restoring my brokenness, with the Word to confess. Luke 1:37 "For with God, nothing will be impossible". Thirty years on, this Word has been my compass and standard bearer perpetually and perennially, as the 'Good Samaritan' Timothy had declared to me.

I first met Timothy very soon after I had lost my wife (Bishop) Diana in 2007. We met at a Christian conference, and immediately engaged in fellowship. Somehow, the Lord led me to share my sorrow with this younger brother, who instantaneously comforted me with his arms warmly around my shoulder, praying touching words that ministered to my grieving soul.

Years later, and now, obedient at 89 years of age, I stand on as the Monk Martin Luther on the promises of God. Since that very first encounter with this man of God, we have kept in touch, and our friendship blossomed. It would be no coincidence that Timothy would befriend my daughter Oweeniya and husband Devan, and later be at Devan's bedside to minister prayers of healing. Again, Timothy would visit, pray and encourage me when I was unwell in Kuala Lumpur.

Stephen Convay said, "Many people are climbing the ladders of success but when they get to the top, they realize the ladder had been leaning against the wrong wall - the same pursuit of King Solomon, wealth, career and pleasure".

After the tragic loss of my family home to fire, we saw countless miracles coming our way. My late wife, Diana saw the birth of the ICAG, - International Christian Ambassadors of God (a council of churches and fellowships), which grew and spread over four continents. In obedience to the Great Commission out lined in the full Gospels, we travelled far and wide spreading the Good News and winning souls. Just as in Isaiah 61.3, the Spirit of the Lord had anointed us to preach the Good News to the poor, lost and needy.

"Make a joyful noise unto the Lord" (Psalm 100).

Indeed, at 89 years of age, standing as a veteran of 50 years in missions I wish to confess reading through Dr Timothy Sng's gift in authorship : "What our Father in Heaven expects of us", that l have fallen frightfully short of the LORD, our Father's expectations as a Christian. Nevertheless, I have

learned and begun to grow in stature over the 12 chapters,
and shall treasure His Word written on the table of my heart
as a beautiful reflection of the Lord's goodness.
I, Eugene remain behind in the Lord's Vineyard, with son
taking over as Archbishop of ICAG, and daughters Bishop
Ujjiniya Pearse & Oweeniya, also in Ministry.
I remain active and vibrant as ever.
I shall end this encomium with
"In Him, I live and, in Him I move, and in Him, I have my
being." Acts 17:28
Yours in His service,
Dr. Eugene Melchizedek Owen
**Patriarch and former Archbishop ICAG, Council of
Churches**
Dip. Tung Ling Bible College, Singapore
Ph.D Missiology Bristol U.K., M.Ed. USA.

PREFACE

This book is written for sons and daughters of God.

Seeking the LORD, while fasting can produce amazing
results.

I had personally dedicated the year 2018 to drawing close to
Father God, and Holy Spirit inspired me to write this title,
literally 'out of the blue!' or unexpectedly.

On one early morning, during a quiet time, this question
sprang up:

"What is it that my Father requires of me?"

The answers came in almost the same sequence as below, needing some rearrangement, and the result being, a new title: "The Good Son."

Here it is, for you and I, - 'What our Father in Heaven expects of us!", and these are some of the criteria that makes you and I - "a good son or daughter", written through the guided inspiration of the Spirit of God.

To keep it short and sweet, the obvious word 'daughter' is omitted in the title; yet she is certainly not omitted or forgotten by our Father. 'Son' is used here generically to mean 'daughter' too.

Culturally, in Asia, there may be a distinction in the role of a son as compared to a daughter; or many may say that daughters are usually naturally close to their parents, particularly the 'father'. The Asian sons are supposed to shoulder the responsibility to care for their aged parents, the so-called 'good son' or 'filial son', refers usually to sheer financial, shelter and material support.

The focus of this book is not from a cultural point of view, though this author is Asian, but from the Christian and spiritual point of view, which is in my opinion, applicable to all sons and daughters, which is 'you and I'.

The good son or daughter's heart is naturally focused on their father or mother's well-being and comfort, - hence also seeking, 'what's best to make father and mother happy'.

Therefore, if God is our Maker, (and we call Him, Father), our hearts should be clearly focused to please our dear Father in Heaven. On earth, a good son or daughter should likewise please father or mother, by 'honoring' them.

A critic will ask, "Why father? What about mother? Is not her sacrifice more? Is not mother more special?"

Of course, mothers are forever special, as the uniquely special and precious one living being on earth, the 'one' who carried you in the womb for a full nine months, the 'one' in whom you totally depended on for your existence and even long after. Mother's precious and timely release ushered you and I into planet earth, thus beginning a life long journey. While still frail, helpless, vulnerable and totally dependent of both mother and father, you grew from day to day, week after week, month after month, under the watchful eyes of dad and mum.

Mother, especially will continue to shower you with love and blessings, all the days of your life, almost undeservedly and without question, as she will always be - your one and only beloved mother!

Mothers will always be placed dearly in one of our heart's four chambers, if not all!

What about our Heavenly Father? The answer again is simple: "He is One and the only One -the Best Father in the world, on earth as it is in Heaven!". And He plays the Majestic Role of both being our Father, and our 'Mother', for all of us came from Him, from ABBA's Heart – El Shaddai.

How then can we not want or desire to please our Father in Heaven? Psalm 42 and Songs of Solomon should be our spiritual anthem, all the days of our life – "to long for Him, and to be love sick for our Father, and to love our Father all the days of our life."

Every living person is a son or a daughter, and many go through life with more than one position or role, even as many as a dozen or more, as a son, a brother, a father, a

husband, a grandfather, a cousin, a nephew, an uncle and
more. Yet, the role of a son or daughter is the primary one in
our character and relationship, because it is in the formative
years of infant, child, toddler and teenager, easily nearly
twenty years of our earlier life that we are in that role of a
'son'.

I believe that when we grow and develop healthily in that
role as a good son or daughter, we will become good fathers
and mothers, good brothers and sisters, good husbands and
wives, good sons-in-law or daughters-in-law, good cousins,
good grandchildren, good step children, good grandparents,
good uncles and aunties, good brothers and sisters-in-law,
and thus a good neighbor and citizen on earth.

This book is about the 'good son' of our Heavenly Father,
and not about being a good son to our parents on earth.

May this little book draw us all very much closer to our
Father in Heaven, as we seek to please Him, as you and I
grow towards being good sons and daughters.

Dr Timothy Sng

INTRODUCTION

Which Son is the Good Son?

Jesus told two parables about two sons.

One is about the often-preached story of 'The Prodigal Son'
found in the Gospel of Luke, Chapter 15 from verse 13

onwards. The other is a short story, found in Matthew 21:28 followed by the question: "Which of the two did the will of his father?"

The prodigal son had requested to be released from all obligations as a son, to be free from his duties and responsibilities, presumably in a busy farm or estate owned by his father. He wanted to be released, so as to be free to experience the world, seek the 'city lights', and live a carefree life of fun and pleasure. He asked for his share of half of his father's inheritance, which would have been a lot of money. The father had obliged and gave freely to his son, accordingly as he had asked and wished, which would have included his inheritance, even half of the father's estate.

Culturally and traditionally, many father's desire and wish is for their sons to take up positions in the family business, and eventually take over, and even taking the company and business to a higher level. For any ordinary father would have been extremely upset and disappointed, if a son approaches him, as the prodigal son did with such a proposition. Very few would allow a son or daughter to demand abruptly his or rights and inheritance. Mostly, the present-day prodigal sons would leave empty handed. Acceding to such a request often threatens the fabric of the family, its unity and harmony, apart from reducing the company's resources into half literally. Yet, this gracious father acceded to the son's request and the story, as Jesus told, recorded that the father gave his 'blessings and consent' allowing the son to go on his way, into the world out there.

This son then went away for some time, living a lavish life, eventually wasting all the cash that he had, i.e. his inheritance over a period of time, whether years or possibly even months. As it all came to 'nothing' or 'zero', this prodigal son ended up destitute and in abject poverty. Left with nothing, he found shelter with pigs and other animals, literally as a homeless vagabond, depending on charity, and living off others for all his basic needs. It suddenly dawned upon him one day, that he would clearly be better off being with his father, if he returned just as a hired worker. With much remorse and regret, he journeyed homewards, believing that at least, he would be granted food and shelter. He did not seem to have any other expectations, least of all to be given back his position and role as a son, as he had defaulted his position when he left home.

To his shock and surprise, his welcome was overwhelming, equivalent to a present day red-carpet reception for him.

From afar, the Father had spotted his long, lost son. Jumping up with joy and delight, he excitedly ran towards the prodigal son, welcoming him wholeheartedly with a loving embrace and a kiss. Moved by his father's mercy and compassion, he repented and confessed his sin, as he instantly regained his status back as a son.

The Father placed an expensive robe, and a ring in the son's finger, receiving and acknowledging him back as a rightful and legal son.

It was definitely a time for great celebration for the Father, as his lost son had returned. He instructed his servants to slaughter the best calf, declaring a big joyous home-coming celebration to announce to everyone, that his son had returned.

All the servants joined in happily in this big celebration of the return of a son, as they too were indeed glad to see the very happy Father, whose great joy was seen in a radiant and beaming face. It was grace and love pouring out from a Father's heart, that became news spread throughout the region. The whole county came to know of this outpouring of 'love' – one of truly mercy and grace.

This story was told by Jesus clearly to describe and preempt the whole scenario of a lost, or unsaved 'soul', having strayed away into the world of sin, yet returning in repentance one day. When in such a contrite and repentant state, our Heavenly Father, who awaits you and I patiently will joyously welcome us into the Kingdom of God, declaring simultaneously a huge celebration in Heaven for every single soul that is safely returned to His Heavenly Kingdom.

But there was one person who was very upset and displeased, as he watched scornfully the whole drama of his Father's excitement. And he was not silent. Instead, he protested in the strongest way, almost immediately, and with absolute disgust and indignation. It was the other son, who had stayed back faithfully over the years to work with the Father.

This angry and jealous second son said, "Father, how can you do this! This rascal of your son squandered all his inheritance, and now returns broke, dirty and filthy. And you give him a huge welcome, almost like celebrating all the terrible things and ways of his life, rather than rebuking him and telling him off!"

"Have you considered that I am here, your faithful son, working day and night for you, and yet never experiencing even once, such a celebration for me? Despite all that I have done for you, Father, I have not even wasted a calf or lamb just for myself."

Obviously, the other son had worked very hard for the Father, and had never left to enjoy life in the world. He was however clearly rude and disrespectful to both his brother and also to his Father by staying away from the celebrations! His whole demeanor or attitude was one filled with anger, and of justice and vengeance, but lacking in grace and mercy.

This reflects the common approach of the world towards a 'brother or sister', unlike the 'agape love' and faithful enduring patience and love of our Heavenly Father towards you and I.

It is correct to say that the prodigal son was wrong, having spent a lavish life in sin. He had ended up destitute, and in that state of despair, he had returned to the Father and repented, expressing sincerity in turning over a new leaf. His return home to the Father was evidence of his repentance, and constituted a genuine change. He did not deserve to be received back a 'good son.' Instead however, he was lovingly received by a gracious and merciful Father.

Calling upon his father by name, yet not demanding any rights was enough for the Father to receive Him back. In fact, all that he had expected was to be accepted back, even if he was to be regarded as one of the other servants. It was his Father, who had graciously lifted him up, and restored him back to his rightful position as a 'son'.

So too, as the Word of God says in the Gospel of John 1:12,13 "But as many as received Him (acknowledged and received Jesus, as Son of God, and Messiah from our Heavenly Father), to them He gave the right to become children of God (i.e. sons and daughters), to those who believe in His name, who were born, not of blood, nor of the will of the flesh, nor of the will of man, but of God (phenomenon of rebirth or being born again by the Spirit of God).

Jesus also related another simple short story of how a Father had called out to the first son to go out on his behalf for a work or project. And this rebellious son immediately replied that he would not go. He however later repented and went. Meanwhile, the second son had said that he would go, but actually did not go. Either he had deliberately lied, or he did not go because he was distracted by other things, or out of sheer irresponsibility and laziness. This latter son did not fulfill his promise to go.

The question that was posed by Jesus was, "Which one is the obedient son? The first or the second?"

They answered correctly that it was the son, who refused initially and subsequently went. Likewise, we can apply the same question to that of the prodigal son and his brother, as to who did the father's will or was the obedient son.

The correct answer is that neither sons, in both stories were perfect. Both faltered and both were flawed. Hence, strictly speaking, neither qualifies as a 'good son.' It is in fact very difficult to choose between one or the other, or as to whether which son is the better son.

In reality, you and I have been there, as we have both been the first son or daughter, or the second, at some time or other in our lives.

We can recall in our own lives, the times when we put ourselves first, and sought after our own needs, rather than that of others; self-gratification, self-satisfaction and self-fulfillment naturally comes first to many, before we consider the 'King of kings', or our father or mother on earth.

That was what happened to the 'prodigal son', who put himself first, rather than the interest of the Father or family first.

The good son places the Kingdom of God first, and is rest assured that all our needs will be supplied by our Father.

While we may not have gone the extremes as 'the prodigal son', we do often fall short, when we fail to put the Kingdom of God first in our hearts.

Can we truly say that it is a life wholly and solely dedicated to God and God alone, rather than a life dedicated mainly to "me, my, mine and my own!"

God, our Father desires that we place the Kingdom of God first in our heart, mind and soul. It is a perspective that will help us prioritize everything in our lives, i.e. God before us, individually. It refers to the inward posture, revealing the desires and intentions of our heart.

This, of course does not mean that one's basic needs for survival is neglected or ignored. As a living mortal being, man like all living creatures, need food for survival, rest and sleep for restoration, cleaning and washing or bathing for good health, and repair or treatment when unwell, apart from having to work to earn a living to provide for oneself and our beloved ones.

Our Father God is omniscient, and can see us, down to a single strand of our hair and or even a single cell in our body, long before the microscope or telescope was invented, or the Internet and Google came into existence.

It is never God's intention to find fault or label the each one of us as good or bad, but it is our Father's desire that everyone respond, repent and return to become a good son, and daughter. (2 Peter 3:9 The Lord is not slack concerning His promise, as some count slackness, but is longsuffering towards us, not willing that any should perish, but that all should come to repentance.)

If then, the correct answer is that neither was the good son, who is? It is fact in that neither you nor I are good. Who then is the 'Good Son?'

The answer is that the Good Son is the narrator of the original story, for He is "The Son of God,"

Someone called Jesus, "Good Teacher". He said with a sharp answer, "Why do you call me good, for only God is good?!"

He did not mean that He was not good, but in fact He affirmed it indirectly. Paraphrased, the answer of Jesus would have been as follows.

"You are dead on target to call me 'Good', because I am the Son of God, and only I, the Lord your God is good, for the Father and I are One, and only We are good."

Let us now humbly come before God, our Heavenly Father and acknowledge the fact that we do not qualify to be called 'good', let alone a 'good son' or 'good daughter', but that our hope is in our Good Father, who is merciful and gracious.

So, when we turn from the world and our sins, and come to our Father in repentance, calling Him ABBA Father, He will receive us back into His arms, as a 'good and faithful son or daughter.'

We may be already a Christian – born again, baptized, Bible-believing and even Spirit-filled man or woman of God, yet we need to be reminded that apart from God or Jesus, we can do nothing (John 15:5), and that unless we abide in Jesus, the Vine, our efforts will be futile.

Will we, you and I do so, today?

Jesus said, "Come, follow Me."

That is the "Call" to all who believe, to become His ambassadors, - to be His `fishers of men'. The call is not for some or a selected few, but for everyone to follow Jesus, to be His believer, His disciple and His follower, to be like Him – the Good Son.

When you and I agree to do that, to believe in Jesus, and to receive Jesus as our Savior, and to follow Him, we have begun on the journey towards being the 'good son and daughter'.

PROLOGUE   Servant or Son

So, what is the difference, whether we are servants or sons/daughters?

Are we actually servants or sons/daughters in the eyes of our Father in Heaven.

The difference is big or huge, - a world of a difference, in fact.

A servant is hired and paid wages, and often employed on a contract. And the contract or work permit has rules and restrictions set out as clear and strict criteria for the 'employment'. The servant has to report for duty at a fixed time, and scheduled to work for certain number of hours, failing which there may be disciplinary actions. Again, from time to time, the servant is monitored, observed and evaluated, to see if the employment can be continued, to decide whether a bonus is warranted, or if the servant can be promoted or should be demoted. There is a constant threat of termination or demotion hanging over the heads of the under-performing servant. On the contrary, the hardworking servant may receive promotions, bonuses and commendations from the 'Boss', though still subject to the rules and regulations of the employment contract.

The servant always looks up to the employer or 'Big Boss' and to the many other little bosses along the way, with submission and respect. Many will bow their heads before their bosses, even kiss the hands and feet (in some societies) of the 'Big Boss', with respect and humility, and out of fear of losing their jobs.

Every servant will feel intimidated in the presence of the boss or 'Big Boss', knowing that their future and well-being depends on this boss, who can literally sack you any time.

Furthermore, whenever the boss or 'Big Boss' arrives or calls for a meeting, the servant has to be prepared or ready to hear for instructions and new rules, often being reprimanded or rebuked. Sure, there are situations when a 'Big Boss' brings in good news or bonuses and promotions, but the fear or worry is always about bad news, and sudden retrenchment. We hear of the latter all the time, even of huge international organizations that go through tough times over the years retrenching hundreds and thousands of staff suddenly.

Thus, servants continue to live under rules and regulations, a law whenever they are at work, and they have to fulfill and abide in these laws. If ever they break these rules or regulations, especially deliberately, they risk being disciplined, reprimanded and terminated.

In contrast, a son or daughter is in a totally different position.

He or she is in a relationship with the Father, with the 'Big Boss'. He or she is the 'Big Boss's son or daughter. It is a world of a difference. He may be on the staff pay role, but he is not a staff in the eyes of the colleague, and even his or her immediate superior would fear him, as he is the son or daughter of the Boss.

A son is ranked as high as the owner, as the 'Big Boss'. And this relationship, even though 'adopted', is unique, permanent and sealed by the Blood of the Lamb, and born of the Spirit of God. It is literally permanent, as long as the son does not falter or deliberately get out of that relationship.

The closeness or intimacy of a son is far higher, deeper and more meaningful than that of a servant and the owner. The son, at work may be considered a staff or employee, but after work, he has dinner with the Father, or 'Big Boss.'

This intimacy is so special that it literally empowers the son to represent the Father, in His absence, unlike the servant who knows his or her limitations in the absence of the 'Big Boss.'

Apart from this intimacy in the relationship, the Father will at different times impart or teach and guide the son to a higher level, often to the same level as he was, with the son taking it even higher.

Jesus said in John 14:12, "Greater works than these he (you) will do, because I go to My Father."

A servant remains a servant and does what he or she is told to do, and can never be elevated to be equal in ability, performance or executive decision making like the boss. The son can be empowered to do so.

Finally, it is love that permeates this relationship, intimacy, and empowerment between Father and son, and when the son

has understood it, "everything that the Father has is for him
to use and control." (Luke 15:30.31)

There is a clearly a huge difference between being servant or
son, and a huge gap between the position, the role and the
ability of the two.

We are birthed into the Kingdom of God as sons and
daughters, born by the Spirit of God, not by blood or by
flesh, nor the will of men, but of God." (John 1:13)

The Word of God is clear that we are rightfully received as
sons and daughters.

2 Corinthians 6:18, declares "I will be a Father to you. And
you shall be My sons and daughters, says the LORD
Almighty."

So, no longer should one live as a servant, but as a son, - a
son who works diligently for the Father, because of His love
for us, and our love for Him. We are elevated to a very high
and royal position, as sons of the Living God.

However, as a son, there is a vital role to play, not as being
under rules to follow, and in so doing, he will please the
Father, and pleasing the Big Boss Himself is all that matters.

We are thus a serving son, not a servant, because a servant
has no rights, while we as sons and daughters are rightful
heirs of the Kingdom of God.

Finally, although we may hear of us being adopted or grafted
in (for the non Jewish people), we are actually not second
class citizens in the Kingdom of Heaven, but equally elevated
as a son or daughter, birthed by the Spirit of God, saved by
the Lamb of God, the Son of God Himself..

(Acknowledgement goes to my senior Pastor Dr Chew for his insight and input that inspired this chapter.)

ONE   Acknowledge & Call Father

First and top on the list is the need to `call' upon God, and to acknowledge Almighty God as your and my Creator and Master of the Universe. His name is 'THE LORD'.

The Bible says in the book of Genesis Chapter 4, verse 26: "Then men began to call on the name of the LORD." This was indeed a great breakthrough for mankind, taking place after the fall of man.

We need to go back to the very beginning, to the time of Adam and Eve to fully appreciate that, man and God were in direct communication from the very beginning. Adam and Eve spoke to God directly, seeing and hearing Almighty God, one to ONE, and face to FACE.

They knew God; they knew that their existence came from God; they knew that God was their Creator and Master; they feared God, honored God, and listened to God's instructions, orders, commands and advice, but faltered very soon after.

God gave direct instructions to Adam that Adam was to be the 'Boss' on earth; all of earth, and everything that existed on earth was at his disposal, use, manage and control. God provided a wonderful and beautiful Garden called Eden, where all the fruits and greens were for him to enjoy freely as food, and he was to tend and manage the garden. Adam, of course represents the human race, and includes woman, though Eve came later. God's instruction was to 'multiply, fill the earth, dominate and rule all the creatures on earth, the fishes in the sea, and the birds in the air.' Man was not asked to rule over each other, and never to kill, steal or destroy, though in the history of mankind, man has crossed way beyond the 'authority' given to mankind.

There were two mystical or magical trees, with special fruits. One tree was called the Tree of Life, while the other the Tree of Knowledge of Good and Evil. God told Adam clearly that he was free to eat of the first tree but not the latter.

God said, "If you eat of the Tree of Knowledge of Good and Evil, you will die." How much more direct or clear can this instruction be? It was like, "Don't you eat from this tree; stay away from this fruit; it will kill you. As for the rest of fruits in the garden, it is all yours to enjoy and eat."

The story goes that Adam and Eve were deceived and they broke the 'Golden Rule' and ate of the second tree. Hence, we are here today, as we are now, in a Post-Adam era, where there is a distance or barrier between God and us. Many still struggle to believe that God exists; atheists will argue that creation is nonsense, and the Charles Darwin's Evolution Theory is the clear answer for the Origin of Man; they reject religion, God and all that goes with faith and belief in the Almighty, even making it an offence to believe and worship God. It is not the intention of this author to enter a debate on the existence of 'Our Father in Heaven.'

Apart from the 'cloud of confusion and unbelief', the whole original arrangement or provision by God for man to have an easy life, with free access to all the wonderful fruits and vegetation for grub changed abruptly. Man had to begin to work and toil for their survival and existence.

Since, we are back to square one, the first thing correct that men did in the Post Adam era, was to restore relationship with God Almighty, described in Genesis 4:26, when men then 'called upon the Name of the LORD.' This was after a period of silence between God and man, with man doing his own thing, and God waiting (patiently and eagerly) for that first call, though we do not know for how long.

Then man called out and acknowledged God, "LORD, LORD, LORD…"

We do not know what happened after that. Did God reply? Did He speak? Did man hear, sense, feel or see anything? Was God silent despite their call?

We do know for sure that it was recorded in the Bible, hence marking the beginning of man's restoration of relationship with God. Knowing our Father's Heart, He was very pleased, that finally 'sons' and 'daughters' acknowledge His Existence and Presence, and called upon His Name.

So too, in our own personal walk and search for a closer, deeper and more intimate relationship with God, our Father. It begins with you and I calling upon God daily, often, and more seriously.

To reiterate, the Word of God says in the Gospel of John 1:12,13 "But as many as received Him (acknowledged and received Jesus, as Son of God, and Messiah from our Heavenly Father), to them He gave the right to become children of God (i.e. sons and daughters), to those who believe in His name, who were born, not of blood, nor of the will of the flesh, nor of the will of man, but of God (phenomenon of rebirth or being born again by the Spirit of God).

In the Book of Galatians, Chapter 4, we read from verse 4-7:

"But when the fullness of the time had come, God send forth His Son, born of a woman, born under the law, to redeem those who were under the law, that we might receive the adoption as sons.

And because you are sons, God has sent forth the Spirit of His Son into your hearts, crying out, "Abba, Father!"

Therefore, you are no longer a slave but a son, and if a son, then an heir of God through Christ.

For that reasons, since we are already sons, acknowledging our Father in Heaven, comes out top of the list of Father's expectations of us – His beloved creation. Until we recognize and acknowledge our Father in Heaven as our God and LORD, we will have difficulty proceeding any further in our relationship with the LORD GOD.

The good son must acknowledge the Father. Do call upon The LORD today.

That is the first thing we do when we enter our biological father's home, whether on a visit after we have left home to enter the world, or when we return from school as a child.

"Daddy or Papa, Abba or Father". We will naturally call our dad or mum the first thing we enter our parent's home.

Jesus Christ, our Lord and Savior was and is the Good Son. He refers to 'My Father' so often, that the Jews were infuriated. They considered it 'blasphemy' for Jesus to call God His Father, thus equating Himself with God. They did not know or believe then, that it was in fact true, because Jesus is the Son of God.

John 5:18 "Therefore the Jews sought all the more to kill Him, because He not only broke the Sabbath, but also said that God was His Father, making Himself equal with God."

That was in fact the real driving force for all of them, especially the Council Members of the Jewish Synagogue to demand the death penalty for Jesus, for in their opinion, calling God one's father is the ultimate 'blasphemy'.

For Jesus, it was natural for Him to acknowledge God as His Father. He said, "I and Father are one." (John 10:20)

The Words of Jesus should not be taken lightly. Meditate on these words in Matthew 23:9.

"Do not call anyone on earth your father, for One is your Father, He who is in heaven."

This means that God, our Heavenly Father – YAHWEH, THE LORD is His Name is Father to all mankind.

In John 17:21, Jesus says, "that they all may be one, as You, Father (are) in Me, and I in You; that they also may be one in Us, that the world may believe that You sent Me."

Thus, calling and acknowledge God as our Father, as your personal Father is so very important – the very first step in life, and the most important call that anyone can and should make.

Call upon God, your Father today. You have a direct line to Him, without any handphone or number to dial. Just look up to the Heavens, with a sincere heart, in a contrite spirit, preferably on bended knees and call The LORD now:

"God. my LORD"

"Father"
"Abba"
"Papa"
"Bapa"
"Daddy"
"Dad"
"Jehovah God"
"LORD, LORD."

Those are His Names, commonly used. When Moses spoke
to God, and wanted to have a glimpse of the Almighty, the
LORD told Moses to hide behind a rock, and He would pass
by. Almighty God knew that His brightness shining
gloriously would be too bright for a mortal being to see
directly.

As the LORD passed by, He introduced Himself as follows:

Exodus 34.6, "And the LORD passed before him and
proclaimed, 'The LORD, the LORD God, merciful and
gracious, longsuffering, and abounding in goodness and
truth, keeping mercy for thousands, forgiving iniquity and
transgression and sin, by no means clearing the guilty,
visiting the iniquity of the fathers, upon the children and their
children's children to the third and the fourth generation."

God introduced Himself. His Name is "THE LORD."

Or in whatever language that you use, your "Daddy" in
Heaven awaits your call, and He will call you, "my son",
"my daughter," if you tune in heart and mind to hear Him.

After Adam and Eve fell, there was a horrible period of
silence between man and God, and man and woman, perhaps
in their severe distress, agony, guilt, shame, sorrow and

troubled mind, body and soul, could not look up to the Heavens, let alone call God, our Father.

Man (and woman of course), are the special species that are upright with head easily lifting up to see the Heavens to rightfully call God, our Father. The animal kingdom and all the creatures have their eyes mostly looking down on earth, and do not have the same status as man, to be able to look up to the Heavens. They know God as their God (Psalm 104), and the fear of God is in them naturally, even as they fear mankind.

So, when Adam and Eve fell, they were estranged and distanced from God. They lost the close face-to-Face fellowship, and stopped calling out to God, until that precious day recorded in the Bible, when men looked up to the Heavens, and rose from their guilt and shame, and began to call upon the Name of the LORD.

The restoration of relationships restarted when "men began to call on the name of the LORD."

This was in fact a momentous and pivotal moment in the history of mankind, when "men began to call on the Name of the LORD."

The acknowledgment that God is LORD, and our Father in Heaven is very, very important, and cannot be overemphasized. Man i.e. mankind must know and acknowledge that Almighty God is God and LORD.

There is no other. With that recognition, comes respect, honor and obeisance to a Mighty God, who is deserving of honor and praise and worship.

When we call God, "LORD, LORD", we are saying that He is the real and true Boss, the Almighty God, to Whom all praise and worship is due.

When we meditate on the truth that God is God, and the LORD is the Almighty God of the Universe, of the Heavens and the Earth, we cannot help but bow down before Him to worship Him.

This author truly believes that all of mankind have the right of access to God, our Father. This author believes that everyone can call upon the Name of the LORD. Do not worry about your status, eligibility or right to do so, - just Call the LORD, because you are from Him, and you belong to Him, and you came from Him. This author truly believes that if anyone is sincere and genuinely cries out to God, his voice will reach the Heavenly Throne.

Of course, as a Christian, we have immediate access to the Holy of Holies. And, if two or more are gathered in the Name of Jesus, He is in our midst. And if we request anything from our Father, and two agree in Jesus' Name, it will be granted by our Father.

We of course know that some prayers are answered instantly, and many are not or are delayed. In the Book of Exodus, we read of the great sufferings of the people of Israel, after the death of Joseph. It came to breakpoint, when their sufferings were unbearable, and they cried out to God. God heard the cries of the suffering Israelites as their voices reached to the Heavens, and God looked down to see their misery.

We also read of passages in the Scriptures e.g. in Jeremiah 14:11,12, where God not only does not want to hear, but turned a deaf ear to some of the segments of society, and even warned others not to pray for the stubborn or stiff-necked people.

Again, in Isaiah 1:15, the Word says, "When you spread out your hands, I will hide My eyes from you; even though you make many prayers, I will not hear. Your hands are full of blood.

We are thankful that we have a merciful and gracious God, and God does not have a black book, and does not blacklist anyone, for as in 2 Peter 3.9, His desire is that all come to repentance and acknowledge Him, so that none will perish.

There is no evil in God, and His mercies and grace are abounding. He longs for his children to call Him, ABBA Father, not at any fixed time or interval, but anytime and whenever.

If at all, our communication lines are cut, it is our fault. Pray, and acknowledge our Father, call upon His Name, and it will be restored. God will hear you for sure, and 'return your call!'

Only believe.

Because we did not pay our phone utility bills, because we kept the phone in the drawers, and because the battery has run out, or damaged, our lines may be cut.

Acknowledge God, our Father, by calling unto Him today. He will hear your sincere call, from "deep to deep", from the depths of your heart, to the Depths of Father's Heart.

"ABBA, Father."

That's the first thing that the prodigal son did when he returned, he called his father, "ABBA!"

Father God immediately 'softens & melts' when we call Him Father, and He graciously welcomes us back into His loving embrace.

Have you called upon the LORD lately?

How often should one call and acknowledge God, one may ask? One major faith requires their followers to do so five times a day.

For the believer in Christ, there does not seem to be a guide, but the practice of giving thanks for each meal would already suggest that one would do so, at least three times before each of the three meals of breakfast, lunch and dinner.

Also, it would also be a good practice to acknowledge God first thing in the morning with the prayer that Jesus taught us, what is commonly called the Lord's Prayer, and in it we are clearly to supplicate for our daily bread, hence a daily commitment.

Finally, a little call to ABBA Father just before night or sleep would sum up the day with thanksgiving and further supplications for the coming days or weeks. With that, it seems acknowledge God our Father several times a day would be the norm; yet this author feels, a once daily call to the Throne Room, to ABBA Father would suffice.

Meanwhile, what about groups, corporations and nations? Many nations include God in their constitution, acknowledging His Presence, and incorporating God in the most important declaration for the nation. It surely does matter, when a nation does so, and declares Almighty God as being Sovereign over the nation.

Call upon God, our Father today, and keep in touch, preferably daily. In acknowledging and calling upon the

LORD, through the Name of His Son, receiving Him as your Savior, you will be immediately elevated into sonship, and be a son and daughter, born by the Spirit of God. (John 1:12,13)

Let us do so now, by reciting from the depths of our hearts, with all conviction in our mind, with all the strength of our souls, this: 'The Lord's Prayer' from Matthew 6:9.

Jesus said, "In this manner, therefore, pray:

Our Father in heaven.
Hallowed by Your name.
Your kingdom come.
Your will be done.
On earth as it is in heaven.
Give us this day our daily bread.
And forgive us our debts.
As we forgive our debtors.
And do not lead us into temptation.
But deliver us from the evil one.
For yours is the kingdom and the power
  And the glory forever. Amen."

So, what does it benefit us, you and I when we call upon our Father: "LORD, LORD."

The principle of sowing and reaping applies. The more you call and acknowledge our Heavenly Father, the more He hears your voice, and is reminded about you and your needs, and there will be more blessings and answered prayers in your life.

For sure, he or she who calls upon the Name of the LORD will be saved.

Also, when you ask (call), seek (keeping calling, while making human and earthly efforts), and you knock (go out and make attempts and work out your projects), while acknowledging Father God as first in your life, you will have a life of abundance.

Keep in touch with God. Acknowledge Him in every aspect of your life.

(The opposite of acknowledging God is to deny or reject God's existence, disbelieving in His existence, and not attributing that all the work of Creation is God's.

The first chapter in the Book of Romans spells out the danger and consequential judgment for those who deny God and His existence.

This author urges the reader to seek God, for by opening one's heart and mind to search for the Living God, you will be found by Him, as God is constantly seeking out for sons and daughters to be returned to His loving embrace.)

TWO   A Grateful Heart

A grateful or thankful heart is so very important. When we realize that literally everything comes from God, and our sheer existence depends on God Almighty, we will definitely need to thank Him every day, and every moment of our life.

After all, "all things were made through Him, and without Him, nothing was made that was made." (John 1:3)

And, Jesus further said, "for without Me, you can do nothing." (John 15.5)

It is therefore natural if not automatic, that we should appreciate God, and be thankful to Him always, for everything indeed comes from Him, and apart from Him, we can do nothing.

Jesus told the story of ten lepers, who were healed, and only one returned to thank Him.

At that time in history, leprosy was a dreaded disease with no cure. Sufferers of leprosy were literally banished for life to a "Lepers' Colony". The Bible tells us of the law, requiring a leper to be covered and to shout out "unclean, unclean" whenever they moved around, so that people would keep a clear distance from them.

In this modern day, many readers cannot truly appreciate what it means literally and in reality, when one suffers from such a dreaded disease. This author was trained in medical school in the early seventies. In the early seventies, in Malaysia and also in many parts of the third world, e.g. India, Africa, there were still in existence leprosy centers or colonies. The Sungai Buloh Leprosarium in Malaysia, was then world famous, as one of the earliest effective drugs for therapy known as "Dapsone" was effectively used there, for the first time. Soon after that, a series of medications were discovered, eventually making leprosy a treatable condition in this modern era.

My teacher at the leprosarium, the late Dr Bhojwani, who has only recently passed away - would literally take our hands and/or our handkerchiefs and rub them on the patients, who were chronic, but healed sufferers of leprosy, to shock and

simultaneously reassure us, that it was a treatable condition.
Later in the late seventies, this author had the privilege to
treat many chronic sufferers of leprosy, some of whom were
severely disfigured with literal holes in their faces, apart from
the coarse and disfigured faces giving them a so-called
'leonine facies.' The holes were caused by erosion of the
nasal and frontal bones, with the nose literally eaten away.
Such was the severity and devastatingly disfiguring disease
of leprosy, if untreated, that the ten lepers knew for sure that
the touch and prayer of Jesus had healed them.

In recent times, barely three decades ago, from the early
1980s, when HIV was just discovered, then called "AIDS" or
Autoimmune Deficiency Syndrome", there was an equally
severe fear and taboo of the disease. This author saw his first
AIDS victim in the United Kingdom in 1985, just four years
after it had been discovered as a new disease. Literally, all
patients with AIDS would perish within three years of the
diagnosis then. The fear and taboo was so great then, that the
nurses in my ward, literally refused to follow the doctors into
the room, unless it was absolutely necessary.

Diagnosing AIDS and informing the patients then was
equivalent to passing a death sentence that read, "You will be
dead in three years." No one then survived beyond three
years of the diagnosis of "AIDS". Each time, I informed or
counselled a patient that he had "AIDS", it was a very
solemn occasion, and I could see a shadow of darkness over
their faces, when the news was told to them.

HIV or AIDS then, can now be treated by medications, with
many patients still surviving until this day.

Back to the time of Jesus, these ten lepers were walking in a
group, when they cried out to Jesus for healing. Jesus obliged

and healed them, in His compassion, as Scripture records that He healed all who came to Him. The healing was not instantaneous though, but was delayed by some minutes. While they were walking along the streets, literally shouting, "Unclean, unclean", as was required of them, by the law, one by one discovered that healing was taking place on their bodies, as they saw their hands and each other's faces being completely healed, and their skins turning normal and pink.

Shouting for joy, jumping up with excitement, they ran off, possibly to their homes to show their loved ones, or to the nearest pub for a beer, extremely elated that they were healed of an incurable disease. They forgot the Healer Himself, except for one of them.

One grateful leper turned back, running to Jesus to thank Him, probably hugging and kissing Him on the cheeks, with tears streaming down with sheer joy! He had been healed by the Master of the Universe. Only "God" could have performed the miracle then. Jesus had to be the "Son of God."

Hear this story again reading from Luke 17:12-19.

Then as He entered a certain village, there met Him ten men who were lepers, who stood afar off. And they lifted up their voices and said, "Jesus, Master, have mercy on us."

So, when He saw them, He said to them, "Go, show yourselves to the priests." And so, it was that as they went, they were cleansed. And one of them, when he saw that he was healed, returned, and with a loud voice glorified God, and fell down on his face at His feet, giving Him thanks.

And he was a Samaritan. So, Jesus answered and said, "Were there not ten cleansed? But where are the nine? Were there not any found who returned to give glory except this foreigner? And He said to him, "Arise, go your way. Your faith has made you well."

Yet, only one returned. On many occasions, when this author reads from this passage or hear a preacher tell this story, the immediate response is that "I am not like those nine!"

However, in recent times, I have come to realize that indeed, most of us have at one time or another been one of the 'nine lepers' in attitude, as we take our healing and blessing so lightly, and went our way, rather than 'fall at the feet of Jesus' with deep appreciation and gratitude.

Pause and ponder again, and meditate on this very poignant story of a miraculous healing, that only one out of ten was grateful enough to return to thank the Master and Healer.

Every story that Jesus told has a deep meaning and purpose for the disciple even up to this day. Leprosy was the 'killer disease' of that day, during the time of Jesus, and anyone healed of leprosy would have been a major testimony, akin to the resurrection from the dead. For a long time since, leprosy remained as the number one cause of nerve paralysis, worldwide, probably only recently overtaken by conditions like diabetes. As recent as 2016, it is still reported that the global prevalence of leprosy was 171,948 sufferers, mainly in India and Africa.

What was obviously 'unclean' had become 'clean', and only a messenger from God could have done such a miracle. To say that the other nine were ungrateful would be probably incorrect, as no one who has been healed of leprosy cannot forget the miracle, or the healer.

The fact remains that nine out of ten did not return, a whopping 90% of them. This figure of ninety percent probably represents the church of believers, that as many as 9 out of 10 of us are guilty of taking our daily healing for granted. God, our Father has healed literally each and every one of us, not just once, but many, many times, in the past, as the Spirit reminds me and you. Can we return to His Feet and bow down before Him in deep appreciation and gratitude and thank our Father for His mercy and faithfulness, in healing us?

True gratitude, a deep appreciation, and a sincere thankfulness to our Lord and Master is so very important, not just for our Father's Name to be glorified, but for our own sake.

A good and regular practice is to give thanks often for all that He has done for you and me. Giving thanks regularly before each meal is thus a wonderful and important practice that most Christians practice.

We can learn from the animal kingdom. We read about the lions, who are one step ahead of us, for they pray before the 'food arrives on the table!' We read in Psalm 104:21 that "the young lion roars after its prey and seek its food from God."

This means that they 'prey and ask' for a successful catch from God, their Master, even long before it is nabbed and 'put on the table'.

God loves a grateful heart, and He is always pleased when we appreciate and thank Him. He is patient and merciful, and waits and waits for years and decades, for all His children to call upon Him, counting and hoping that one by one, they would repent and return to the Father's Heart.

The story of the prodigal son is not focused just on the son, but also emphasizes the Father's loving and patient heart, waiting for each son and daughter to return.
2 Peter 3:9 says, "The LORD is not slack concerning His promise, as some count slackness, but is longsuffering toward us, not willing that any should perish but that all should come to repentance."

To God, our Father, all sons and daughters are lawful and rightly sons and daughters, mercifully forgiven and just awaiting their return (repentance), and are automatically welcomed with great celebrations in heaven.

Thanksgiving, or Thanksgiving Day is celebrated every year on the fourth Thursday of November in the United States of America, since 1789, beginning with the first President, George Washington.

The proclamation of a national day of "Thanksgiving and Praise to our beneficent Father who dwelleth in the Heavens" was made by President Abraham Lincoln.

Could it be that a nation that includes God in its constitution, and proclaims a national day of thanksgiving and praise to God, our Father, - could that be the main driving reason for Almighty God to continue to protect and bless America as a great nation, when so many great nations from the time of early civilization, whether Egypt, Iraq, Spain, Poland, Germany or even Great Britain have one by one suffered seasons and years of hardship, and undergone crises after crises.

Let us continue to have a heart of deep gratitude, with thanksgiving all the time to our Father in Heaven, for God is good and there is no evil in God.

He is the Mighty Provider of all things, and we cannot thank God enough for so many things that He has done for mankind. There is an endless supply of oxygen, water, vegetation, and food, and it is God who provides, not 'Mother Nature.'

From the richness of the earth, which is God's spring forth literally huge trees, and resources and material to build sky scrapers, buildings for officers and homes, as well as all the advanced electronics from cars to gadgets. Man's intelligence taps on God's generous provision, and the whole world continues to develop and progress in an amazing pace.

We may shout out that "we are the captains of our souls and the masters of our fate", and it is true up to a certain point. We need to think, plan and act to make skyscrapers materialize, but until we believe, trust and acknowledge that it is all by God's grace and provision, all that we build can collapse in seconds.

William Ernest Henley quote of being 'the master of my fate, and captain of my soul' is true only to a certain point, and in the context of the need for human effort, wisdom and direction, under God's guidance and direction.

Neither can one boast that "I am a self-made man!" or that "I did everything myself!" Really, truly, so? Have one forgotten that the first 9 months, you were a total parasite and fully dependent on your mother in her womb? And after that, for a good many more years, as an infant and toddler, you were fragile and dependent on mother, care-givers, nurses and others for your survival?

No one can truly be independent and self-made, and hence must always appreciate that we have arrived because of other people, and give credit to others, especially God Almighty, your Creator and mine. John Donne's quote is true of man, that "No man is an island!"

Jesus told the story of such a `boastful, self-made' man in Luke 12:18-21.

"So, he said, 'I will do this: I will pull down my barns and build greater, and there I will store all my crops and my goods. And I will say to my soul, "Soul, you have many goods laid up for many years; take your ease; eat, drink and be merry."

"But God said to him, 'Fool! This night your soul will be required of you; then whose will those things be which you have provided?'

"So is her who lays up treasure for himself, and is not rich toward God."

It is perfectly fine to be rich and successful, for as Jesus said that the poor will always be with us, so too will there be rich and successful people.

The key is to be thankful, to give thanks to God for our success, and to share our wealth, and tithe to God, for being generous is one positive way to show one's gratitude for our success.

"For what profit is it for a man, if he gains the whole world, and loses his own soul." (Matthew 16:26)

Let every son and daughter be forever grateful for each one's salvation, which has elevated each of us from the depths of darkness, and from captivity to be set free and raised up as a child of God.

By the saving grace and mercy of our Lord Jesus Christ, we are now born of the Spirit of God, and granted eternal life. The Lord is our passport and Pass-Word (Passover Lamb & Word of God) to enter heaven, and our names are written and sealed in the Book of Life, when we call upon Jesus as our Savior.

For that alone, we must be eternally grateful to our Father in Heaven for His love for us.

With an attitude of gratitude and thanksgiving, we can be contented and at peace with God and men, and all the negative aspects of dissatisfaction, discontentment, dispute and disharmony will be thrown out from our lives.

You will then truly realize that "God is good, and there is no evil in God", and "God's plans and wishes for you are always good", and hence if things do not turn out well for you, it is neither God's fault nor necessarily yours. Instead, you take up a posture and attitude of always and forever giving thanks and praise to God for His goodness, and you will begin to see things turn around.

Read books by author Merlin Carothers e.g. "Prison to Praise", "Power in Praise" and "Praise Works."

The truth is that there is no evil in God, in so far as His plans for you and I, and also there is no such thing or phenomenon as 'chance', for even in the drawing of lots or numbers, God is there to determine the answer, as we know of it as a practice in Old Testament, when they pray and draw lots.

If then, chance does not exist, there are only three or four factors that contribute to outcome in life, i.e. "God" through His Divine influence, "you" through your choice and plans, if God does not change it, "other people and the situation, if God allows it", and finally "the enemy or prince of the earth who is out always to steal, kill and destroy", if God allows it, and does not nullify it.

God, your Heavenly Father is working, all the time through your angels and mine, and through the whole Army of God, for your well-being, for the whole earth to function flawlessly and in perfection, until the end of the earth.

Floods, typhoons, hurricanes, volcanic eruptions and earthquakes take place as God has planned and allowed, and as a sign of the End Times, of the return of Jesus. Of course, the master of disruption, the one who steals, kills and destroys will rise up to do damage whenever there is opportunity.

The books of Jeremiah and Job both relate on the interaction of the LORD and the enemy over one's lives, and the reason behind it.

Jeremiah 27:6-8 "And now I have given all these lands into the hand of Nebuchadnezzar the King of Babylon, My servant; and the beasts of the field I have also given him to serve him. So, all the nations shall serve him and his son and his son's son, until the time of his land comes; and then many nations and great kings shall make him serve them. And it shall be, that the nation and kingdom which will not serve Nebuchadnezzar the king of Babylon, and which will not put its neck under the yoke of the king of Babylon, that nation I will punish, says the LORD, with the sword, the famine, and the pestilence, until I have consumed them by his hand.

The LORD had declared that the people of Judah will serve under the harsh King of Babylon, and the prophets had prophesied otherwise, but God in His mercy at a later time came to save Judah from the hardship and suffering, and Nebuchadnezzar himself was punished.

Jeremiah 27:22, "They shall be carried to Babylon, and there they shall be until the day that I visit them," says the LORD. "Then I will bring them up and restore them to this place."

Thanksgiving, gratitude and praise is a posture and attitude for the son, at all times, in all situations. Job did not fully understand why he was going through all that turmoil, tragedy, and personal sickness, but he kept believing and trusting in a good and loving God, and in the end, the trials and tribulations ended.

Spend good quality time, on bended knees, and head to the ground in true, sincere worship of God Almighty, our Heavenly Father, and express with all our heart, our mind, and our strength our gratitude and thankfulness to God for all that He has done for us (individually for yourself & collectively, your family members, friends, colleagues and mankind).

When we truly have a grateful heart and express it from time to time, even daily rejoicing and giving thanks to a faithful

God, there will be a transformation in your life, in your relationship with our Father in Heaven.

The principle of sowing and reaping applies. Blessings come and favor shows up on you and I again and again; do we stop saying "Thank you", because we have already said so. What is the sincerity, seriousness and depth of our thanksgiving? Can one expect to keep receiving, favor after favor without gratefulness or even a sign of reciprocation?

So, thankfulness and gratefulness must surely be more than just an expression from our hearts and our lips, but translated into acts of blessings and deeds to others. To quote the Book of James, faith without works is 'dead'. Therefore, our gratitude is made alive and sincere, when we please God, our Father with good deeds from a grateful heart, blessing others as a sign of our gratitude, because He has blessed us.

So, thanksgiving and a grateful heart will ensure that blessings and favor will continue to flow from our Father, who sees our gratefulness.

(The opposite of gratitude and appreciation is in fact one of complaining, ungratefulness and a murmuring heart.

In one instance, they had complained so soon after having witnessed God's miracles which had set them free from the tyranny of Egypt. They visibly saw how the mighty pursuing Egyptian army perishing in the sea, while they had passed on the dry bed of the sea. This had provoked God's wrath, and Moses had to intercede and plead for them, resulting in God mercy, sparing their lives from destruction.

We read the story in Numbers 14.2-18.

Verse 2: "And all the children of Israel complained against Moses and Aaron, and the whole congregation said to them, "If only we had died in the land of Egypt! Or if only we had died in this wilderness!"

Verse 3: "Why has the LORD brought us to this land to fall by the sword, that our wives and children should become victims? Would it not be better for us to return to Egypt?"

Verse 10: "And all the congregation said to stone them (Moses & Aaron) with stones. Now the glory of the LORD appeared in the tabernacle of meeting before all the children of Israel."

Verse 11: "Then the LORD said to Moses: "How long will these people reject Me? And how long will they not believe Me, with all the signs which I have performed among them?"

Verse 12: "I will strike them with the pestilence and disinherit them, and I will make you (Moses) a nation greater and mightier than they."

Moses interceded appropriately, and the LORD agreed with Moses and spared their lives.
Nevertheless, for all their grumbling and doubt in God, God decided that none of that generation should enter to see the Promised Land, as all of them perished by the end of their journey in Sinai. They paid the price and never saw the Promised Land.

In another situation with Joshua, the complaining and murmuring had progressed to rebellion in Korah, and the judgment and penalty for rebellion was demonstrated swiftly, when God's wrath acted and the ground under the rebelling families opened up and swallowed them in.

If one had read those passages casually, one may think that murmuring or grumbling is a small matter, and many Christians `grumble' and `complain', even in church if the air-conditioner is too cold or not cold enough, if the music is too soft or too loud, if the sermon is too short or too long, and many more reasons for their discontentment, but one thing is clear: "Grumbling or murmuring is the exact opposite of gratefulness and thanksgiving, and is an unhealthy, rebellious, evil attitude and practice.

Dear Christian, grumbling and complaining should stop. Instead, praise and give thanks all the days of your life, for God is good, all the time.)

THREE   Obedience

Obedience is plain and simple, yet very deep in its significance.

The son obeys because God is a good God, a good Father, and He knows best and we are to do His will for His Glory and for the Kingdom of God. It may sound painful, but that is the right and best thing to do for a son – a good son.

Many righteous and devout men or women of God would want to put obedience top on the list of our Father's desire or wish-list for a good son. This author felt, possibly guided by the Holy Spirit that the first two simple steps of 'calling out to Father God' and being 'grateful' would catapult us much nearer to Father's Heart, and pull upon His strings of mercy, before the trials and tribulations that are associated to 'obedience' comes into play.

We have no problems coming before a great King and Master, and falling at His Feet, in worship and praise. We have no problems even in bringing our King a special gift of sacrifice to show that we love Him.

But, the Word of God is clear, "Obedience is better than sacrifice."

1 Samuel 15:22 says, "Behold, to obey is better than sacrifice."

God has laws, statutes, commandments and ordinances, and He directs us to follow and obey them.

Christians always swing between the "Law" and "Grace", often with severe arguments and conflict between two groups, one for and the other against, using scripture to quote their preference and inclination.

The best scripture must surely be the words of our Lord Jesus Himself, for He is the WORD.

He says very clearly in Matthew 5:17, "Do not think that I came to destroy the Law or the Prophets. I did not come to destroy but to fulfill."

Do you and I think that Jesus fulfilled the Law of Moses, or the Ten Commandments? Did He break any of the Ten Commandments?

The answer is clear. Jesus did not break even a single one of the Ten Commandments, though by virtue of being the Lord of the Sabbath, He overruled that particular Law to save lives on the Sabbath.

Why then the Law?

The Law of Moses was necessary before Grace through Jesus Christ came, and the Law reflects God's righteousness and holiness.

The first five Commandments are about mankind honoring God, and His representative on earth, - our parents. The next five Commandments are about honoring others, apart from ourselves, and around us - our neighbors.

If honoring is difficult, it is because we do not love; if there is love, then all that is in the Law is achievable. That is a clear affirmation again that the greatest of all the commandments or laws is "love", as Jesus Himself confirms that this is the first commandment.

Matthew 22:36-38

Verse 36: "Teacher, which is the great commandment in the law?"
Verse 37: Jesus said to him, 'You shall love the LORD your God with all your heart, with all your soul, and with all your mind."
Verse 38: Jesus said, "This is the first and great commandment."

If you love the LORD, you will have no other Gods before
the LORD (No.1), and you will not make any molded
images as gods (No.2), nor will you take His Name in vain
(No.3), and you will keep a special Sabbath day holy without
work to spend time with the LORD (No.4), and hence finally
naturally, you will honor your parents (No.5), - if and when
you truly love the LORD.

Likewise, when you love your neighbor, you will not kill
(No.6), nor hurt them with an adulterous relationship (No.7),
nor steal from them (No.8), or lie about them (No.9), or be
jealous and envious of their assets, spouse or anything or
anyone they own (No.10).

If and when you truly love your neighbor, you will not do
anything hurtful and painful things towards them, and hence
keep the law (Ten Commandments), from No. 6 to No. 10.

So, as Jesus says, He came with love, to show love and to
bless us with His LOVE, by laying down His Life. He
fulfilled the Law during His Life on earth.

God, our Father wants us to obey these laws, which are not
binding, not suffocating, but in fact liberating when we truly
love. Jesus came to set the captives free, and if anyone is
trapped with hate, anger and evil intentions, they will easily
break all the Ten Commandments.

Jesus came to set the captives free, and He liberates us from
our evil past. Why go back to our 'sinful' and 'evil' past. In
reality, all the Ten Commandments are easily broken,
especially when scolding equates to murder, and looking
lustfully with the eyes is adultery. Many if not all, would
have done either or both, in our life time.

Likewise too, it is just as easy, as stated above to fulfill all the Ten Commandments, when we have love, and have the love from God in us.

Obedience means to follow the law and not to do evil. One will follow and worship only God, our Father, and not follow other Gods, or we will do evil towards one's neighbor by stealing his wife, stealing his assets, lying, or being envious over the neighbor's riches.

Obedience means to live a holy and righteous life.

Why then do we need Grace?

We need grace, so that, when we fall and do wrong, we will not perish but by His Mercy, we are allowed to rise up again from sin and death, for the wages of sin is death.

Romans 6:23, "For the wages of sin is death, but the gift of God is eternal life in Christ Jesus our Lord."

Sin is not a part of Christian life and living. Grace is, and being above or fulfilling the Law is a natural thing. Besides, grace is vital in the Christian walk, because we will always need grace to forgive others who have wronged us, in one way or other.

Grace is given to enable us free and easy entry into Heaven, without being judged, (for we have all sinned against God) and 'Grace' also enables us to rise up higher above the natural law and common sense, to forgive, and love our neighbor, even though they have sinned against us.

Grace is available for us, not only to be forgiven, but also so
that we can live in repentance.

Titus 2:11,12 says that "For the grace of God that brings
salvation has appeared to all men, teaching us that denying
ungodliness, and worldly lusts, we should live soberly,
righteously, and godly in this present world."

When there is love, and love for our Father, you will not only
obey Him and His laws, but more than that, you will treasure,
keep and love His Words, His Laws, His Commandments,
His statutes and His ordinances.

When we truly love God, and love Him with all our hearts,
and all our mind, and all our soul and all our might, we will
find 'obedience' a natural and most automatic thing. For all
that you and I will wish to do, is to please Him, even as you
adore and worship our Father.

Many little children will promise daddy and mummy that
they will follow us and do anything that we ask them to do,
in their innocent little hearts, before the world corrupts them.

The path to obey and follow may be difficult initially, but as
it becomes a natural part of you, it is in fact an effortless and
easy way to walk the righteous and holy path to follow God.
That is the way that any good son or daughter will choose
and follow – in His Footsteps.

There is also the clear call from God, when we hear from
Him to do what He directs us to do, as was related in the
introduction on the story of the two sons.

The best example perhaps is in the Book of Jonah, on Jonah's story. He was a prophet, and he knew God, and he heard directly from God.

Interestingly, he was 'called' to go and preach to the city of Nineveh. Nineveh then, was among the largest cities of the world, almost as big and famous as Babylon. God loved the people of Nineveh, and desired that they repent from their sins, and return to Him. Thus, He sent Jonah, a very famous prophet of that time. And God chose Jonah and Jonah alone. He was the prophet that God wanted to use, to preach to the city of Nineveh.

God always chooses the best, and the right person to do the job. Likewise, God has chosen you for the situation and the task that He has decided to act upon. Will you go?

For you family, your neighbor living beside you, and your colleagues at work, you are the best person, Hand-picked by God, to be His spokesperson.

Jonah refused to go. He disobeyed, and then did something that was deliberate and naughty. He ran away. He literally ran away from God. He jumped on board a ship, hence taking him further away from Nineveh, testing God with his open, flagrant disobedience. His actions spoke clearly, "No, I am not going!"

We read later, the true reason why Jonah refused to obey. It was because he knew that God would not punish or destroy Nineveh, but would show His Mercy, after he had declared judgement on Nineveh. In fact, it was so graphic that Jonah, after he had declared judgment on Nineveh, had gone up to a hill, waiting at a vantage point, presumably to see first hand the destruction of Nineveh. The prophet did not want to lose 'face' if his prophecy did not come to pass. He had declared that there would be fire and brimstone and his prophetic declaration was serious and frightening. The king immediately repented and ordered all the people to repent, wearing sack cloth and mourning.

God loved Nineveh, and He longed for the hearts of the peoples to change, and of course, He knew that the king would respond to Jonah's prophetic word. God's divine plans had worked. He chose Jonah, as Jonah was the prophet that the people feared and respected then, as a 'voice from God.'

Thus, God made a huge storm that terrified even the most seasoned seamen. From captain to the lowest ranked seaman, they knew that it was a serious storm that would bring down their ship, if they did not act. They threw literally everything over board into the sea, hoping that a lighter ship would not sink, an act that is desperate and a last resort for any captain. It did little to still the storm, that continued to rage violently. It made every seaman go down on their knees to pray and cry to their gods.

It was that bad. Jonah was the only one on board who did not do anything. He was in fact, sound asleep in the storm, ignoring the rocking and rolling, belligerent and stubborn. His actions spoke clearly again, "No, I am not going."

One of the stewards going through the ship was shocked to see Jonah fast asleep, and proceeded to wake him up, rebuking him for being asleep, when he too, should literally be on his knees praying for his life.

That was the man of God and prophet, Jonah! He was downright disobedient, and a very brave man indeed to face off with God.

He was nonplussed and cool, when he confessed to the
steward frankly, that he was the cause of the harsh storm, and
it was God who was shaking the boat relentlessly. He went
on to state that the only way to calm or still the storm, was to
throw him overboard into the sea.

What a courageous prophet, with pinpoint accuracy in
hearing from God, and stubborn faith that God would not
allow him to drown even in a dark sea. The seamen knew
indeed then, that this was a man of God, running away from
the Almighty, and though they feared doing so, they had no
choice but to eventually throw Jonah overboard.

Jonah was right. The storm ceased immediately. And God
send a big fish, - a whale to swallow him. And in the belly of
the fish, swirling away, with weeds entangled around him, in
total darkness, after a few days, Jonah finally repented and
agreed to go and preach to the city of Nineveh.

He had paid the price for his disobedience. He lost to God,
and submitted finally. His arguments with God did not stop
there. You can read all about that in the Book of Jonah.

The story ends with a deep message of God's love for the
people of Nineveh, which is present day Mosul, of Iraq. We
do not know what happened to Jonah after that, as the chapter
ended, though the comic series of Beano or Dandy continued
to portray him wrongfully as a jinx, who sinks ships by his
mere presence on board. This is of course not true, because
no ship was ever sunk because Jonah was on board. I believe
Jonah ended up a governor, if not the official prophet of
Nineveh.

In recent years, following the severe assault and eventual takeover of Mosul by ISIS, the population of Christians in Nineveh shrank to zero, or nearly so.

The moral of the story is that, we cannot win or go against God's wishes. If He calls you, it will always be a blessing to go; if you refuse, and object and disagree, then you will face more challenges, and in the end, you will still be persuaded to go. And when you finally go, it will truly be blessings and open doors, for being 'obedient' to Father God is always the right thing to do.

Obedience, when you hear from God, is the key God's covering and blessings over your life.

Obedience is clearly the better 'narrow path', when compared to the wider path of ignoring, avoiding, disobedience that leads to rebellion and destruction.

Deuteronomy 28.1 clearly tells us that, "if you diligently obey the voice of the LORD your God, to observe carefully all His Commandments which I command you today, that the LORD GOD will set you high above all the nations of the earth."

This is affirmatively followed by Deuteronomy 28.2. "And all these blessings shall come upon you and overtake you, because you obey the voice of LORD your God."

The Voice of the LORD our God, is none other than His Living Word, the Scriptures, or THE HOLY BIBLE.

Read for yourselves the blessings upon blessings in that Chapter if we obey, and the opposite outcome, if we disobey.

It may be tough, or it may be a struggle, and we can do so on our knees, but the outcome is clear, that it is necessary and far better "to obey the LORD God, our Father and Master."

The perfect Son of God struggled too, and obediently followed the Master Plan of our Father.

In Matthew 26:42, Jesus, the Son of God said, "O My Father, if this cup cannot pass away from Me unless I drink it, Your will be done."

And, we thank our Lord Jesus that Jesus went to the Cross of Calvary for you and I, in total obedience and submission to our Father.

Let us love the LORD for all that He has done for us, and because we love Him, we will follow and obey Him. Trusting and obeying go hand-in-hand, for when we trust Him, we will obey, knowing that He will give us the strength and peace to overcome and rise up for His calling.

What is the benefit or fruits of obedience? Again, the principle of sowing and reaping applies. Being obedient and obedient, time and time again, means that one can be trusted and depended upon.

In real life, the teacher or instructor will allow you to move on to a higher and more advanced level, because you can now be trusted to take on higher tasks.

So too, from our Heavenly Father, for now you have passed the test and can move on to more and more tasks. And being the Good Father, He never sends you out without blessing you with special and necessary anointing, or empowering.

David had passed the test of obedience in looking after the flock and God had empowered him with the strength and ability to overpower lions and bears.

Thus, Goliath was no problem for David, and God chose him out of all the soldiers, and he was promoted to 5-Star General and soon after, as king.

Obedience will thus lead you to 'promotion' and 'empowerment' and in due time 'exaltation' before God and men.

[The opposite of obedience, is clearly 'disobedience', which is sin and a crime, the best example perhaps being that of Adam and Eve's fall. And we are all paying for what the wrong that Adam and Eve did in the Garden of Eden. God will not easily say, "Never mind, you are forgiven."

It is this author's experience, that whatever we do, there will be repercussions, and these repercussions are real and they return sooner rather later, like a boomerang, especially when we sin or disobey.]

FOUR   Drawing Near to Father

Father God loves us so much, so dearly that He loves all His children to come into His Presence, to draw near to Him, to be at His Feet, and even sit on His lap, in close embrace, even to lean on His Chest, and hear His Heart Beat.

This intimacy is a very precious one, and is a natural thing to do, when you and I love God, our Father "with all our heart, all our mind, all our soul, and all our might."

Not only would we want to draw near to Father God, but to remain there, to stay there in His Presence, for hours and hours and hours.

Any infant baby would prefer to be in the arms of the mother or father, especially the suckling child, when hungry, longs for the mother's breast. This intimacy is indescribable for both mother and child and illustrates and epitomizes this intimacy that we, as God's children should long to be in.

That is in truth, our first love, to be close to Daddy, ABBA Father, from whom all of mankind come from.

A child, seeing the 'Daddy' come home, just as soon as the doorbell rings, would run to 'Daddy', and 'Daddy' would joyfully grab son or daughter, lifting the child up into the air, and say, "Daddy loves you!"

Likewise, as 'Abba' is sitting down in the living room sofa, either reading newspapers or watching television, the child runs in and jumps on to 'Abba's' lap, and 'Abba' delightfully drops the newspapers, embraces the child, kissing lovingly the cheeks and declares again, " Papa loves you."

This drawing near to your 'Daddy', - this special intimacy and relationship of being close to 'Papa', is so natural and mutual a relationship, between father and child, - a special or unique bond, that is in fact the 'main thing' which is often missing in many Christian's walk with God.

This author cannot claim or say that he has arrived at this special relationship of divine intimacy. We can call it entering God's Presence, being in His Presence for charismatics and Pentecostals, or being in the Eucharistic Adoration in the Catholic Church; it is entering into a special intimacy with the Lord.

One needs to dedicate time to be in God's Presence, or drawing near to the LORD. In one's so-called 'busyness' even doing good Godly work, one should not neglect setting aside time for this precious duty or responsibility of being still in God's Presence.

They may be Godly Christians, truly God-fearing, and law-abiding, serving Father and Master diligently and full-time, but yet do not spend enough quality time to be close to Father God. We can often be so busy doing 'God's work' and forget the main thing, which is to draw near to Father, to be at His Feet, especially when He desires us to be near to Him.

I recall vividly reading Reverend David Watson's testimony recorded in his book, "Fear No Evil". It was a privilege to have met Reverend David personally, when he spoke at an evangelistic meeting in Birmingham, the United Kingdom in 1981. Reverend David was already an established evangelist in the United Kingdom, and his ministry was spreading to the United States, when suddenly, he was diagnosed as having cancer of the colon.

He testified in his book, how he struggled with the LORD, protesting to Him and the doctor that he had a busy schedule lined up in the USA. Of course, all those meetings were cancelled, so that he could undergo surgery and subsequently chemotherapy.

His struggles ended when peace came, as he heard clearly
from the LORD at a later stage of his illness, and I quote and
humbly paraphrase here:

"David, all your activities serving Me, even your being busy
travelling in ministry is not as important as your relationship
with Me. It is you that I want as I long to have fellowship
with you."

It struck him like a thunder bolt, as he suddenly saw the
perspectives of ministry and travel, and his underlying
sickness. He surrendered totally to the LORD, and peace
came to him, a special peace beyond all understanding, as he
related in his book.

James 4:8 says it very clearly, "Draw near to God and He
will draw near to you."

What is more important in life than God? We know that apart
from God, we can do nothing; yet with God, all things are
possible! Thus, it is best to be near God, as near as possible,
and it begins with us, you and I making that move to be near
to Him.

A few clues may suggest that one is declining in our intimacy
with the LORD, and hence drifting from our Master Creator
and Father.

Have you ever heard the voice of God, speaking to you
audibly, whether softly or loudly? If not, then draw close to
Father, and you will hear Him, feel Him and experience His
love. Talk to Him; ask Him questions; speak earnestly to
Him; communicate knowing that He is hearing; imagine that
you are in His Presence, your eyes closed, on bended knees,
and keep speaking to our Father in Heaven, and you will

begin to sense and know the difference. It may not be days or weeks, and it may take months, even years, but one thing is sure i.e. when you deliberately and actively draw near to God, you will find Him there ready besides you, as He has promised in His Word, and His Word is true.

Do you struggle to feel God's Presence? You wonder and ponder, and get restless because you have no feeling about His Presence. Is your faith more at head or mind level, rather than heart, chest or belly level? Read again the Word of God in Psalm 16:8 and Matthew 28:20, that He is at our right-hand side, and that He is with us always till the end of time.

It is like a love relationship, or marriage relationship, where strangely, both spouses hardly communicate, and neither feel the "oomph", and intimacy has become a struggle.

It is time to draw near to Father, and stay there until you know that He is there beside you, with you, and around you.

Often, and naturally, when you begin to say you want to draw near to God, nothing significantly happens. You go on your bended knees, and call upon the Name of the LORD. Then, you think or say: "I do not feel anything."

Not yet, naturally. But, God hears, knows and He sees. All your petitions and cries and prayers have reached out to the Throne Room of Heaven. Keep pressing on in prayer. Maintain the posture of trust, belief and assurance that you are indeed drawing close to God, our Father.

The truth is that Father loves us so very much, that He desires us to be close to Him, and all for our own good.

It should be so to for us to reciprocate, but yet, it is so often not so, even in this author's life. A few years ago, this author decided to spend three precious weeks with the LORD, flying off to a secluded mountain village and resort in the highlands of Borneo, a beautiful town called Barrio, where the Kelabit race of North Borneo in Sarawak live. Just before the plane took off, right in the tarmac, as the engines of the plane started revving up, a deep sense of remorse swept through my heart that it had taken me so long, to take this special break, a 'honeymoon with the LORD', in fact. Imagine, after a few decades into marriage, the bridegroom realizes that he had not yet taken his bride for a honeymoon. That was exactly how I felt, as tears streamed down my cheeks.

As a deer pants for the living waters, so our heart should seek after God. Just as a nursing baby or infant, a child or a toddler, seeks and longs after their mother, not once in a while, but all the time, we too should seek after God, our Father, in whose Presence, we are complete and contented.

Indeed, when we are in God's loving presence, we will have everything, and hence, "shall not want." (Psalm 23)

God, our Father is our source of everything, and it is only natural that we should desire to draw near to Him, seek after Him, long to see Him, and meet Him, face to Face.

When we are deeply in love, we want to be near our beloved, and when we are apart, we fall sick – or become love-sick. Like in the Songs of Solomon, we long to be with Him, and declare that "My beloved is mine, and I am His." (Songs of Solomon 2:16)

Seeking God, our Father is so very important for all believers, because "Salvation" is only the beginning of a deeper relationship and friendship with God. We start off by waiting upon Him, and spending our quiet time with Him. Just merely setting aside time for God is an important step towards drawing close to Father. Father knows, He hears, He sees and He will delightfully respond and reciprocate, when we delight in Him.

David Watson, in his book "Fear No Evil" described his struggle or battle with cancer of the colon. He was struck down with cancer at a time, when his ministry was expanding and he was due to go to America for a few weeks stretch when his doctor told him that he had cancer, and needed surgery and chemotherapy after that.

His initial ʻarguments' or conversation with God, our Father, was full of frustrations and exasperation, because his schedule was so tight. He had argued with God that "he could not afford to fall sick", being so busy serving Him. Due to his sudden illness, he had to cancel all those meetings that were already scheduled to go on for weeks, including engagements in the United States.

He related how at the end of his struggle, he heard from God, paraphrased below:

"David, all your meetings, engagements and busy programs for evangelism and preaching the Word, is not as important as ʻyour relationship with Me.' It is you that I long to spend time with. He surrendered to God, and found peace.

At the end of the day, it is not us seeking God, but God seeking us, and longing to have quality time with us. God, our Father came down almost every afternoon to have tea with Adam and Eve. It must be His favorite hour. He came down one afternoon, looking for Adam and Eve, but they could not be found. They went hiding. God called out to them with His clear booming 'Voice', and Adam replied behind the bushes, sheepishly and shamefully.

"We are naked!"

Imagine, special guests, in the form of your King or Queen, are right there in your living room, calling out to you. The King and Queen have come to your home to visit you.

But you could not come out, because you are both naked, and have no clothes to wear. God discovered (of course, He knew) that Adam and Eve had sinned, and after His initial wrath and judgment, our Father graciously wraps the first couple in leather, freshly sewn, and sends them back into the world, to face all the challenges in the world, as a fallen man and woman.

The LORD GOD, our Father seeks to have fellowship with us, when we wait upon Him, and be still before Him. He longs for us to draw close to Him and seek Him, as any father would too, and it is He who comes close to us.

Frequency too, is important. Is once in a while, once in a long, long time sufficient? Do you visit your parents only once in five years? Certainly not? Once a year? Once a month, or every week? Some faiths demand that the follower prays up to five times a day. The Word of God says, "Pray without ceasing" for when we pray, we are speaking to God, and through this constant communication, we will draw close to God, especially when sincere all the time.

Intensity and devotion matter too. Mary Magdalene drew close to Jesus, as a servant to the Master, which some critics wish to distort. Thus, when Jesus sat down to teach, and

Mary did so too, at His Feet, it upset her sister Martha, who was focused on the necessity to prepare dinner for the Master and the disciples.

Naturally, she complained to Jesus. And Jesus replied aptly in Luke 10:42, "But one thing is needed, and Mary has chosen the good part, which will not be taken away from her." In fact, Jesus had rebuked Martha, though Martha was busy trying to prepare dinner. Jesus said, "Martha, Martha, you are worried and troubled about many things" followed by the verse above.

The chapter ends there, but I believed Martha too got the message, and sat down and listened. That night, they had dinner late, and it became 'supper', as the Master Himself began to teach.

Jesus said that one thing is needed, and we should go for that one thing, - the main thing, and that is the Master Himself.

There was a young rich man, who was faithfully listening to Jesus teach. Recorded in Matthew 19:19 onwards, Jesus was teaching about the need to honor one's parents and to love our neighbor as much as ourselves.

This young man declared, "All these things I have kept from my youth. What do I still lack?"

He had posed the million-dollar question to the Master and Owner of the whole Universe, and he was about to get the billion-dollar answer for mankind.

Jesus said to him, "If you want to be perfect go sell what you have and give to the poor, and you will have treasure in heaven, and come, follow Me."

Hearing that, the man went away sorrowful.

He had missed the point. Even if he was the richest man on
planet earth, the greatest of all is to love the LORD, and here
in front of him was the LORD Himself, who is offering
Himself to the young man, by inviting him to follow Jesus.

After all, it is Jesus that matters and when one is with Jesus,
you do not need anything else. There is no need for riches, no
need for property, no need for name or fame, because the
Master of everything is there for you.

If we draw close to our Father, we will have everything that
we need. In fact, when our Father is pleased, He will come
and stay with us.

In John 14:23, Jesus answered and said to him, "If anyone loves
Me, he will keep My word; and My Father will love him, and We
will come to him and make Our home with him."

Drawing near to God is the same as 'intimacy' with God.

Intimacy and drawing near to God involves all our senses, all
our effort and energy. We are reminded again that it is the
first command, to 'love God with all our heart, all our mind,
all our strength and might and all our soul.'

Our senses are sight, hearing, feeling (touch), smelling
(aroma and fragrance) and tasting – and we can indeed
engage God with all the above senses, being mortal. . Yet, we
can go beyond the above senses and enter the spirit realm,
and engage in the spirit, through prayers, prayers in tongues,
sharpening our senses with fasting, praise and worship.

Next, intimacy is about romance and love. Romance and love are about language, action, deeds, and expression. It is the same in our romance and intimacy with God. We need to express our love to our Father, and say it the way we know best, reminding us and Him of what He has done for us, His love for us, and declaring our love for Him, drawing near into His embrace, and kisses, listening to Him, and longing for Him, often in tears of joy and from the depths of our heart and spirit being.

Dreams, visions and hearing the audible voice of God, sensing His Presence, the weight of His heaviness, and knowing that God is with you, in your midst, all contribute to your journey of intimacy with God.

It is a special love relationship with our Maker, and He hears and feel everything that you say or do. It is more than bringing gifts and sacrifice before God. It is you and I that God, our Father dearly desires, our time, our dedicated time at His feet, at His bosom.

In one camp, when this author was speaker, on one afternoon as we were preparing to invite His Presence, bringing palm leaves (equivalent of laying the red carpet), and waiting upon Him, two of the members of the camp were slain in the Spirit.

One of them, a young adult in his twenties and a young boy, about ten both testified that they were brought up to Heaven. The young boy experienced great joy and peace as he related seeing streets of gold and precious stones, and testified that the gold was transparent as he could see through it.

The young adult did not see anything but was held in the warm loving embrace of the LORD. He felt such peace, joy and sense of security that he felt complete and joyful in Father's loving embrace.

That was evidence for the campers and speaker that God had visited us in the camp. The topic of the camp being, "The Good Shepherd and His sheep."

Intimacy is friendship, courtship, romance, love, and takes up to a higher level of closeness to God. Monks and nuns who spend hours and hours in prayer and in adoration know that there is no better place to be than to be in God's loving Presence, away from the world but in His Presence.

What is the benefit, purpose or fruit of drawing near to God? What a silly question? In presence day language, "what's in it for me?", or what is my profit!

When we are near to God, close to His chest, highly favored by Him, next to Him, as intimate friends, and He is the Almighty God, the Maker and in charge of the whole Universe, is there a better position than that?

[The opposite of being intimate or drawing close to Father is being distant or aloof. God, through His Son has now called us His friend, individually.

John 15:15, "No longer do I call you servants, for a servant does not know what his master is doing; but I have called you friends, for all things that I heard from My Father, I have made known to you."

Now, God has extended His Hands of friendship in more than one way. He has in fact done the absolute act of

friendship in giving (not offering) His Son on the Cross of Calvary, dying and paying the price of ransom for our sins.

John 15:13, "Greater love has no one than this, than to lay down one's life for his friends."

And if God our Father has gone the extra distance, the ultimate act, in fact of friendship for us, what then is our response?

When one is distant, aloof with disregard, even ignoring or putting aside our Father, as we would to people whom we consider as not 'close friends' or even enemies, but distancing ourselves, we are literally deliberately staying far away from our Father.

And it is only when these ones are desperately in need that they cry out to God, and when they are still in despair, they complain that God has not answered their prayers.}

FIVE   Undivided Loyalty

Eastern culture emphasizes a lot on the son being filial, and loyal to the parents.

This teaching is translated into the role and responsibility of the child to look after the elderly parents, when they are sick and frail. This duty or responsibility falls on the son, more than on the daughter, though the daughters seem to naturally flock to look after their parents, when they fall ill or are elderly.

One Asian nation has in fact made it law for the children to look after their parents. The often-heard story is the children packing off their parent or parents to the old folk's home, against their wishes. While this is not necessarily a bad or evil thing, in the context of the developed world, where society and individuals concerned accept the fate that when ill or elderly, the children cannot possibly look after them, and they then willingly check into a 'center' or 'resort' for the elderly.

The Taoist religion take it a step further, and worship or prayers for the deceased parent or parents become another obligation and practice, i.e. the belief that a filial son should set up an ancestral altar for worship and even sacrifice of food to their deceased parent or parents.

Bible believing Christians do not support this practice of worship of ancestors, but fully support respect and honouring of our parents all the time, as it is one of the Ten Commandments.

Loyalty or undivided loyalty to our Father, the LORD GOD is very much more than that. It is a total and complete commitment and devotion to Father God. It is a denial of all other Gods, and declaring that there is no other God, but the LORD. This is the first commandment of the Ten Commandments that God wrote on the tablets for Moses to bring down to the people of Israel and it remains as the Ten Commandments to this day.

There is no room for dependence, belief, following or trust in any other beings or gods. The Bible says that we can worship one, either Mammon (money) or God. Our hearts cannot be divided between God and riches.

The analogy is closely drawn to a sacred marriage, where any desire or lust for any other person apart from the spouse will constitute adulterous thoughts, and when it becomes a deed, - an evil adulterous relationship out of wedlock has occurred. There is no allowance for any marriage, traditional ones under the law of Moses or of Grace, where you can freely kiss, hug, love or engage in any sexual acts with another, other than with your spouse.

Strictly speaking, any form of thought, act or deed or flirtation that is sensuous and sexual towards another, apart from your spouse has crossed the line.

Undivided loyalty is the same, when one's heart seeks after other gods apart from the LORD. Our God, our Father in Heaven is a very jealous God, and He will not tolerate any other God in our life. The reason why that is so is very clear, for it is for our own good that we do not follow after other Gods, but only follow after the LORD alone.

God our Father wishes us to have undivided loyalty to Him, and Him alone for these very valid reasons, and it is always for our own good.

It is clearly stated in the First Commandment. "I am the LORD your God, and there shall be no other Gods before you."

When you have the LORD as your God, you are complete and you have everything, and there is no need for any other God. You should invite Him to be your LORD, and declare that there is no other Gods before you. If you have not yet done so, - remember that He is the Almighty, the Creator of the Heaven and the Earth, that henceforth truly, you do not need any other gods. Your eyes, your heart, and your mind should love and seek after the LORD GOD only, and never stray to other gods.

Father God wants you and you alone as His precious child, and will not share you with any other gods. The LORD God is a jealous god, like all spouses, who should never share their intimacy that is reserved and dedicated for each other only, but never with others. It is an absolute thing, no matter what one may thing.

If one allows a little bit of room for sensuousness, flirtation, or anything contact that is sexual, it will become an opening that will lead to an adulterous affair. A touch, even an eye contact, a light hug, a flirtatious word between colleagues, or between boss and staff is enough to act as a spark that may become a wild, raging, uncontrollable fire. Even the strongest of man or woman can fall in temptation, and many have fallen helplessly and hopelessly from a holy pedestal into a path of sin and of shame.

Moses had led the Israelites out of Egypt in a painstaking and miraculous way, and they had seen the Hand of God, through the many miracles, about a dozen of them, one after another, before they were truly set free. They knew that God was the LORD, and He was powerful and awesome and supreme, above all other Gods.

They had fled for their lives in the night, when Pharaoh finally reluctantly agreed to let them go, but he changed his mind soon after, and send the army in hot pursuit.

They had reached the banks of the Red Sea, and could see the Egyptian army approaching them from a distance. They were terrified.

So, Moses cried out to God and sought God for help. Once again, God performed yet another mighty miracle, as he used Moses to split the Red Sea, just by raising his staff or rod in faith. The waters were parted, and a strong wind blew and made the bed of the Sea dry up. The people passed through safely, and as they had just crossed over, the Egyptian army arrived and followed into the dry path.

The LORD closed the waters behind the Israelites, drowning the army and the horses, as chariots also went down under. It was a mighty and awesome miracle that saw a victory, well beyond the imagination and understanding of the Israelites.

The children of God were now safe across in Sinai, free from slavery, and now no longer under any form of bondage. God summoned Moses up to the mountain to meet Moses. God had been a faithful and awesome God to them, without question, and all of them had just seen and experienced the manifest works by the majestic Hand of God.

Yet, no sooner as Moses had gone up to meet the LORD, just a mere forty days away from the people, as Moses entered God's Presence in the sanctuary of Mount Sinai, when the peoples' heart went astray. It can be as easy as that.

They had demanded Aaron to make them a golden calf so that they could worship it! Aaron, the priest strangely agreed and did as they requested.

This happened while God was face to face with Moses, and writing down the Ten Commandments on two tablets. God was furious. God's wrath was translated instantaneously to Moses, who in his anger threw down two sets of precious tablets written by God's own fingerprints defining the Ten Commandments.

Apart from this first horrible act of an adulterous people, more than once throughout the journey in Sinai, Moses had to intercede for the unfaithful people of Israel, as God's anger and wrath was provoked. In yet another instance, God declared that He would destroy that generation, and when Moses interceded with the Words of God our Father Himself, declaring that the LORD was merciful and compassionate and loving, God's wrath abated and He turned away from His intended judgment. We read it in the Book of Numbers, 14:18,

Moses had in his meeting with the LORD in Mount Sinai requested for permission to see the LORD, to which the LORD had instructed that he wait behind a rock and that the LORD would pass by. When the LORD passed by, showing His Glory and Shining Brightly, He introduced Himself to Moses.

Exodus 34:6, "And the LORD passed before him and proclaimed, 'The LORD, the LORD God, merciful and gracious, longsuffering, and abounding in goodness and truth, keeping mercy for thousands, forgiving iniquity and transgression and sin, by no means clearing the guilty, visiting the iniquity of the fathers upon the children and the children's children to the third and the fourth generation.' "

Moses urged the LORD to have mercy on the people, when God's wrath was provoked and God wanted to destroy the Israelites because of their stubbornness and disloyalty. Using God's exact words describing God as we read in Numbers 14:18, God relented and forgave.

Numbers 14:19, "Pardon the iniquity of this people, I pray according to the greatness of Your mercy, just as You have forgiven this people, from Egypt even until now."

Numbers 14:20-24, "Then the LORD said: 'I have pardoned according to your word; but truly, as I live, all the earth shall be filled with the Glory of the LORD, because all these men who have seen My Glory and the signs which I did in Egypt and in the wilderness, and have put Me to the test now these ten times, and have not heeded My voice, they shall not see the land of which I swore to their fathers, nor shall any of those who rejected Me see it. But My servant Caleb, because he has a different spirit in him and has followed Me fully, I will bring into the land where he went, and his descendants shall inherit it.'"

The people had been disloyal and though God spared their lives, they were not allowed to see and inherit the 'Promised Land'. Only Joshua and Caleb, of those who left Egypt made it to the 'Promised Land'. Thus, the people of Israel wandered around the deserts of Sinai a total of forty years, perishing one by one, until all had died, before Joshua and Caleb crossed over the River Jordan, with the new generation of young Israelites. This is very sad indeed,

This example is the best and most striking example of disloyalty, mercy and grace and judgment from the LORD.

Loyalty, faithfulness and not accepting any other Gods, is translated similarly to marriage, where there is no room for any other lover, intimate friend or even part time or temporary God or partner. That is how strict and serious God's expectation is of his children.

God reciprocates with a very strong and assuring promise
and commitment to us that He is faithful and does not fail us.

Hebrews 13:5, "I will never fail you nor forsake you."

Because the LORD is faithful and He promises that He will
never fail us nor forsake us, God expects the same from us –
to be faithful and loyal to the very end.

What then is the benefit of loyalty or undivided loyalty? The
answer is obvious, for the rewards are great. When one walks
with God all the way, with unfailing loyalty, no turning back,
there is no doubt that the blessings and reward, at the end of
our life, when the final battle is won, we will receive the
victor's crown.

**[Sadly, the opposite of undivided loyalty is turning away
from God, and it leads to death, and punishment by
rejection from God, unless repentance takes place before
judgment. For that reason, we must guard our salvation
with trembling and fear of God.]**

SIX   Kindness & Mercy

It cannot be understated that the LORD expects you and I to
be kind and merciful.

God, from Day One, when He made Adam, and then Eve
gave man a powerful mandate to "multiply, to subdue and
dominate" the earth, to rule over all the creatures and animals
on earth, and to have full access to all the fruits and greens,
which were meant to be our food.

We were and are to be in full control of everything, - we were the Boss, over all creation, except over other men, or women, who are our equals.

With this authority, comes power and with any form of power there will always be the possibility of abuse or misuse. We have read in the Old Testaments of good kings and bad ones, and we have seen in recent times, leaders who rise up to be dictators or benevolent ones, the former being more common.

This is the nature of man and woman, that when we are in power, in position of authority, when we are rich, in control, and when we are 'Boss', the tendency is not to be kind and merciful, but to be harsh, bossy, authoritative and even unkind or cruel.

This author believes that God knows the heart of man, that man is corrupt and evil since the fall. It was as early as in Genesis 6:6 that God 'regretted' making man, and even decided to destroy all of mankind.

We read in Genesis 6:6,7: And the LORD was sorry that He had made man on earth, and He was grieved in His heart. So, the LORD said, 'I will destroy man whom I have created from the face of the earth, both man and beast, creeping things and birds of the air, for I am sorry that I have made them."

This is a very strong and tragic statement. It is equivalent to a parent, a father or mother telling a child that he or she regrets having given birth to the child, and now has decided to extinguish the breath and life from the child.

At first reading of this last paragraph, we will be shocked, as we have often been shocked by stories of infanticide and murder-suicides. Yet, this was what Moses was inspired to write and hence recorded in the Book of Genesis.

Thanks be to God, Noah lived at that time, and God's little "Experiment' called "Project Earth" was allowed to continue till today.

Genesis 6:8,9, "But Noah found grace in the eyes of the LORD. This is the genealogy of Noah. Noah was a just man, perfect in his generations. Noah walked with God."

Other versions say that "Noah found favour with the LORD", and "Noah was a righteous man, blameless among his contemporaries."

It may be true that it is impossible to be 'perfect' as a man, but one truth from this and other verses about Abraham, Enoch, Zechariah and perhaps a few more is that "we can be perfect and righteous in the eyes of God."

Thus, with such power and authority that God has given to you and I, it is very important that "kindness and mercy" be blended into our hearts so that we do not seek vengeance and justice, but always grant mercy, for "Vengeance is for God to mete out."

There was indeed plenty, and the Garden of Eden must have been and probably would still be the most beautiful garden in the world. He however set one rule, and that was to avoid the Tree of Good and Evil, for if Adam disobeyed, it would be fatal.

Adam and Eve were deceived and they ate of the Tree of Good and Evil and fell. Man's eyes were opened, as they fell in sin, and suffered the harsh judgment that came, for the wages of sin is death.

God's mercy came in, as His wrath fizzled away. We read even after the harsh judgment was said, God made cloths of skin to cloth both Adam and Eve, the first set of cool leather wear.

God's redemption plan began to operate, and a few thousand years later, the Savior in the form of the Son of God, Jesus came down on earth, lived and mingled with His Creation. After three years of amazing ministry revealing Himself as the Son of God particularly to His disciples, work was completed with the final act on the Cross.

Jesus went to the Cross of Calvary, laying down His Life on the Cross as a ransom for all, paying the price by His own blood shed, washing away all the sins of mankind once and for all. Our Father in Heaven saw that, and thus the Heavenly Gates were opened for man to return and rest for eternity with our Father forever.

The door and path for mankind back to Heaven, for all who believe in Jesus and that Jesus is the Savior of the world, sent by the Father.

Jesus declared that "I am the Door", and "I am the Way the Truth and the Life. No one comes to the Father except through Me." John 10:9 and John 14:6

Prior to that, there was no possible access to enter the Holy of Holies, except through strict criteria and strict preparations. Only the high priest could enter at an appointed time, once a year.

God, our Father, in His Kindness and Mercy forgave all mankind of sin and punishment, when He gave His only Son as ransom or substitute for all our wrongdoings.

The path of Grace was opened and mankind became a new creation, enabling man to shed the `skins and garment' of hate, murder, bitterness, rivalry, strife, envy and jealousy. We were set free, because Jesus came to set the captives free.

Now, would God, our Father now condone and allow the 'evil' nature to continue in man when 'Grace and Mercy' has already come freely for mankind?

Kindness and mercy are the very important acts that come from a heart of love and compassion. The world is full of cruelty and evil, and is in fact an already a 'killing field', where murder and hate have dominated for centuries and centuries. The whole earth is soiled and stained with blood, sweat and tears of men and women, who have perished from and under the evil of their fellow beings, often unjustly so. Man or woman thus has no right to take the life of another fellow being.

Acts and deeds of kindness and mercy will reflect our Father's Heart, and hence will be very pleasing to Him.

The Bible exhorts us to visit the sick, give to the poor, take care of widows and orphans and be kind to the foreigner. Of course, loving one's neighbor is part of the great and first commandment, and neighbor means everyone near to us, and even far off.

Anything apart from kindness and mercy to others would be against the heartbeat of God. How can anyone say he loves God, when he or she hates his or her neighbor?

Consider this: if all of mankind is kind and merciful, the whole world would instantly change, and be a better place.

There would be no more wars and strife. There would be no hunger, as the rich and plentiful would feed their neighbor. There would be no crime or killing, as all will love each other, coexist in harmony. There would be no cruelty to your neighbor, and even the pets, animals and stray ones will be looked after and fed. There would be no oppression of one's neighbor and hence the foreigner would be well treated. There would no need for policing and security, as murder, stealing and violence would not exist. There would be no need for lawyers, courts and judges as there are no conflict and no cases to deliberate on.

Even hospitals would shrink in size, and sicknesses will decrease and decline naturally, as the earth is blessed and slowly cleansed of sin and blood.

It is only obvious and natural that 'kindness and mercy' are indeed very important criteria for all mankind to exhibit and live out in our lives, as the Living God, our Father, who is in Heaven truly expects it of us? The Lord's Prayer says it clearly, that as we ask Father God to forgive us of our sins, we should likewise forgive others who sin against us.

Let kindness and mercy begin from within one's heart. For a start, be kind to yourself and your loved ones. Next, share and spread your kindness to your friends and colleagues. After that, go one step further to show kindness to the poor, the orphans, the widows, the sick and even the foreigner.

From there, you will soon be able to show kindness and mercy to all.

When you show kindness and mercy to someone, you do so to the LORD. Matthew 25:43 says, "I was a stranger and you did not take Me in, naked and you did not clothe Me, sick and in prison and you did not visit Me.

Being kind and merciful does not mean that you have to give away all your money, or even opening your homes to everyone all the time. Yet, you will naturally want to give and share your love, resources and funds with those who are lacking.

Kindness and mercy have to be lived out, when one goes the little extra distance to help someone in need, especially when you see it or when that person comes to you, and seeks your assistance. Turning away someone who knocks on your door for a glass of water or some bread is an evidence being unkind and lacking in mercy.

If someone has harmed or hurt you, and you retaliate and hold a grudge of bitterness against that person, then you lack mercy and kindness.

You need to be kind and merciful and the right thing to do, would be to forgive, and embrace your aggressor with love and compassion, overriding and overruling the natural tendency to seek vengeance.

Remember, "Vengeance is the LORD's", not yours or mine.

We see this verse as a strong reminder for all, quoted three times in the scriptures i.e. Deuteronomy 32:35, where it first appears, followed by Romans 12:19 and Hebrews 10:30.

Romans 12:19 says, "Beloved, do not avenge yourselves, but give place to wrath; for it is written, "Vengeance is Mine, I will repay," says the LORD.

Can you not be kind and merciful? Is it so very difficult to share and give just a little to assist someone in need? Have you not considered that the Son of Man, Jesus came down to earth to die for you and I, suffering a painful death on our behalf, so that we can have everlasting life?

Try it today. Begin to be kind to each other, and slowly but surely, you will see the peace of God enter your life, bringing love, joy and peace, and all the other fruits of kindness, i.e. goodness, faithfulness, gentleness, longsuffering (patience), and self-control (temperance) become naturally a part of you. (Galatians 5:22)

The WORD of God is strong and clear, that unless we forgive, our Heavenly Father will also not forgive you.

Jesus said in both Matthew 6:14 and again Matthew 18:35 clearly this important principle.

"For if you forgive men their trespasses, your heavenly Father will also forgive you."

"So, My Heavenly Father also will do to you, if each of you, from his heart, does not forgive his brother his trespasses."

Being kind is so important, and gentleness, love, compassion, and mercy are all linked to this great gift or fruit of the Spirit, which is in you. It may be, that as an infant and child, or even in your teenage and adult life, you have been badly treated and, a revengeful, angry and rebellious tinge or nature develops within you.

Kindness does not mean giving up your everything for your neighbor, but to have thoughts, feelings and actions for your neighbor, who is in need, who is down, and who is helpless, sick or in pain.

Kindness also comes from a position of strength and authority, exemplified when your towering 200-pound frame faces a 99-pound weakling in a face off. We are a mere speck of dust if we are to appear before God. In our sinful state, we cannot even stand before the Almighty, whose brightness is overwhelming to the sinner.

Our Father in Heaven is very kind to all of mankind, and He expects the same degree of human kindness towards others, especially our fellow being, who is weaker.

A believer who is unkind, lacking in compassion, not showing mercy, in my opinion is only one step away from being a 'cruel and evil' person, and deserves a total shake-up, a re-formatting or re-booting before, he or she can be called a 'new creation' in Christ. Amazingly, it is the Holy Spirit of God who does this awesome work within us, so that we become born again in the Spirit, and a new being is birthed within us.

In this author's opinion, based on membership in several local churches, at least in three countries, that 'kindness and compassion' is generally lacking in the Christian community, i.e. in the church, even in many pastoral staff, and that is something that pains the Father. Judgement will fall upon all who are guilty, unless they (we) repent and change before God.

More often than not, the majority of believers belong to the brother of the prodigal son, who would chase out, disregard, ignore and certainly not welcome or celebrate a believer, who has sinned, when he returns to church. Even the best of believers would be suspicious and cautious of any fallen believer who has repented, even sometimes banning him or her from taking office for a life time. It was Barnabas who opened his heart to welcome and fellowship with Paul, when he had just come to know the living Christ.

Honestly, how many of us would propose that the church welcome a thief who ran away with half of the church's monies, when he returns broke and bankrupt, repenting for his error, after a few years in jail, to rejoin the church? What if the 'thief' was the pastor or shepherd of the church? Would you welcome him back as your leader, pastor and beloved friend, without any reservations?

"Dear Mr or Ms 'Goodson' or 'Gooddaughter', if we are to look into the mirror and view our heart, our mind and our inner being, can we see an image that reflects our Father's Heart – one of kindness and mercy, love and grace.

Can we put ourselves in the shoes of our Heavenly Father and run to receive the 'Prodigal Son' who is returning?

Whenever we are in a stronger position, or in a better situation, whether rich, healthy, or on higher ground, remember the weaker, the disadvantaged, and the suffering, we should do something to assist, help and alleviate the other's suffering. We may be in a stronger position to help, save or heal someone. Just do it!

The saying is clear, that between 'mercy and justice', choose mercy.

We can begin by little deeds of kindness and mercy, a little by little, day by day and the heart of mercy and kindness will grow.

If we meditate on the loving kindness and mercy of our Savior Jesus, and see His merciful and compassionate 'Sacred Heart', there is only one option for you and I, but to do the same, and be kind and merciful.

What are the benefits or fruits of being kind and merciful? As we sow more in this area, you and I will be more and more kind and merciful, for we begin to understand God's love, mercy and kindness, and appreciate those around us who are weaker, poorer and less fortunate.

The main benefit for kindness and mercy is that when our turn comes, and when some painful situation takes place in our lives, we will experience God's kindness and mercy flowing in through our lives.

Do we need our Father's kindness and mercy? This too is a silly question, for everything in our lives is totally dependent of a compassionate and kind God and Creator.

[The opposite of kindness and mercy is obvious. It is being cruel or unkind, showing no mercy.

The cruelty that man has committed to his or her fellow being is documented in history of mankind, with endless acts of genocide, some still ongoing. Many nations were

born from such acts of exterminating the weaker race
and taking over nations and even continents.

Man is totally depraved, and often worse than the animal
kingdom when we consider the despicable acts that
mankind has committed on each other.

The torture, the murder, the rapes and annihilation of
thousands and millions of innocent fellow men, often done
deliberately, systematically and with unthinkable evil
justifies man's eternal punishment. Literally the whole
earth is stained and contaminated by the blood of men,
through the evil act of man.

At the first murder, when Cain killed Abel, the curse on
mankind, or the curse on the earth, through its
contamination began. Even then, punishment was not the
death penalty, as the LORD provided a refuge and
protection, marking Cain so that he would not be killed,
for revenge is God's priority.

Man has not stopped in the evil that man is capable of
doing since that day. In the history of mankind, we read
in the Scriptures of at least two situations where God had
to act. The first was the great flood, a judgment that was
meant for all of mankind, but because Noah found favor
with God, mankind and the animal kingdom was spared
of total elimination.

The next judgment that we read about was in Sodom and
Gomorrah, where fire and brimstone fell and destroyed
the whole city, very much like a modern day nuclear
bomb, for even as Lot's wife looked back, the brightness
turned her into a pillar of salt.

Our Father in Heaven, in His mercy and grace has granted to all of mankind salvation, in the Name of Jesus, as all have now already been redeemed and bought for a price.

Will you and I continue to be uncaring and not helpful to the poor, the sick, the orphan, the widow, the foreigner, for in not giving, not helping or even under compensating them, or even being unkind as pay masters, when they work for us, or in respect to any of the above, through our unkind deeds or neglecting to do good, you and I are being cruel or evil.]

SEVEN   Good Stewardship & Diligence

Jesus told a few parables about the good and bad stewards.

A steward is a manager, a person of authority, with power over people and assets. This power and authority have been conferred or granted, either temporarily or even for a life time to the steward by the original owner or boss. The owner or boss is away, either for a long period or for short periods.

This indeed is relevant to almost everyone or every living being on earth, as all of us have been given authority and power, at least on our own lives, with time and our own energy at our disposal.

It is the choice, attitude and implementation or actions that will differ from person to person, and ultimately, each and every one of us is accountable. Even as a servant or slave (in those days), you have to be a good steward of your time, for everyone will be accountable.

The good son or good steward is one who will use this authority and power the same way the owner or boss would, with kindness, with fairness and with responsibility. He or she acts on behalf of the Boss, and should do so in the same way that the Boss would.

Our Father is the owner and boss, and He is a good Boss.

In the Kingdom of God, there are many positions, and all of them are honorable, respectable and good.

Firstly, we are sons, and our sonship is Spirit-based as we are now born of the Holy Spirit of God. We are also royal priests, kings and prophets, especially in our homes, as we take on the role to be a good father or mother.

We are appointed God's royal representatives, or 'Ambassadors of Christ', representing God literally in every area, for which reason we are called 'Christians'. Whatever you and I do, say, even think (if they can see our hearts and read our thoughts), will be perceived as exemplary of our role and behavior as a Christian.

1Peter 2:9, "But you are a chosen generation, a royal priesthood, a holy nation, His own special people, that you may proclaim the praises of Him who called you out of darkness into His marvelous light."

2 Corinthians 5:20, "Now then, we are ambassadors for Christ, as though God were pleading through us; we implore you on Christ's behalf, be reconciled to God."

1 Corinthians 6:19,20 "Or do you not that your body is the temple of the Holy Spirit who is in you, whom you have from God, and you are not your own? For you were bought at a price, therefore glorify God in your body."

These three verses should tell you and I, who we are really, as a believer in Jesus Christ. We are highly positioned, highly exalted, and very powerful. Our deeds, and actions matter a lot, and make a great difference.

Yet, the best description of our role is that of a humble servant and steward.

In the parables and in real life situation in the Bible, we hear that all authority and power is at the disposal of the steward. Joseph when he was made the Prime Minister of Egypt was all powerful and second only to the Pharaoh. Anything that Joseph said goes, or is law, and hence implemented and executed. He was accountable only to the Pharaoh.

Likewise, Daniel and all the other stewards or chief servants in those days were in charge, and Bible says that everything was under their control and authority, even though they too were servants. When the Master went on a journey, these stewards were in full control, making all decisions, at their own discretion.

Thus, as the parables of Jesus relates, told by the Lord Himself, there were good and bad stewards. The bad stewards were cruel to their underlings, beating or physically and mentally abusing them. One common trend was that these bad stewards would literally change and turn nasty the moment the Master has left, thinking that the Master would not be back so soon.

Journeys of those days, unlike the present supersonic age, may take ages, from months to even a year or two. Marco Polo's travels to China and back, on horseback, with mules and donkeys as entourage would take months. So would the sea voyagers like Vasco da Gama and Albuquerque.

Meanwhile, the bad steward is creating havoc at home. Many a time, the owner returns suddenly or prematurely, and catches the steward sleeping, drunk or absent. The penalty would be severe, as the responsibility granted to the steward was total, including the trust – total trust in him or her.

Similarly, our Master is away for now, until His Second Coming, and it has now been a good two thousand years, and since He is not back, we are in charge of our lives, and "we can lead our lives" as we wish, so-to-speak. And, we can treat our underlings as we wish, "so-to-speak." The Master is absent for so long, that many have now became doubtful that "the Master exists", even to the point of becoming an atheist. There are yet others, many in fact, who may believe that there is a Master of the Whole Universe, but lives a life feeling that he or she has the full freedom to do whatever he or she desires, not bothering about the consequences of the Master's judgment.

Yet, in reality, we are all accountable. We are accountable for our lives. We are accountable for our families, for our work and tasks set before us, our funds and monies, our assets and our precious time, and as bosses, accountable to manage our servants and staff under us.

How do we spend our time, our energy, and our resources? How do we manage as a worker? How do we manage as a parent, as a brother, as a son, as a daughter? How do we use our funds and assets at our disposal, all of which are not really ours, but belonging to our Master and Boss, though fully at our disposal?

Above all, how do we treat our servants and workers under us? God, our Father is watching and He knows. He sees everything, and the angels that watch over us, also report to Father God. Do not be deceived to think that all your hidden secrets and mine, can be hidden from God, our Father.

We have to be a good steward, and a good boss, for He is definitely going to take stock when He returns. Meanwhile, His angels are keeping record. The Boss, our Father knows, and is not sleeping; neither is He deaf, dumb, blind or motionless.

When He returns, in this case being the Second Coming of Jesus, we have to meet Him and are accountable to Him. Some, if not all in the generations before us, have already returned to Him earlier, and have faced the Supreme Judge.

Will He pat us on the back and say that we have been a good and faithful servant, or will He rebuke us?

The answer is simple: Be a good steward. All that is under you, even if it is in your name, is actually not yours, but only under your care, and disposal as a steward.

Be a good steward of Father's things, for He has put it in your hands for your good stewardship, and you are accountable to Him, the Master when you meet Him. If you truly love your Master, and you truly know Who He is, His nature and personality, you will be a good steward, almost naturally.

Firstly, be a good steward of your own life. Ask yourself, as this author often asks of himself, how you are doing as a steward of your own life. If you and I put God and His Kingdom first, we will always want to please our Father and do things that pleases Him – this being the seventh of a dozen things that would please Him.

Watchman Nee, one of my favorite authors, has a life motto, which goes like this:
"I want everything for my LORD, - nothing for myself."

That is the right attitude for everyone, so that we would live and steward our lives for His Glory and to please our Father. Many of these stewards in the Bible do not have a name, yet during their life time, they were in charge of all that was under them, often everything that the boss owned.

We read in the story of Abraham in Genesis 24:1,2 'Now Abraham was old, very advanced in age, and the LORD had blessed Abraham in all things. So Abraham said to the oldest servant of his house, who ruled over all that he had, "Please, put your hand under my thigh, and I will make you swear by the LORD, the God of heaven and the God of the earth, that you will not take a wife for my son from the daughters of the Canaanites, among whom I dwell; but you will go to my country and to my family, and take a wife for my son Isaac."
'

This servant ruled over all that Abraham had. Even the task of finding a wife for Isaac, Abraham's heir to everything depended on the steward or servant. Such was his position and responsibility, and if he had slacked, it would have changed the course of history of Israel.

Next, as a parent, elder sibling with authority over our children and some ways over our young siblings, apart from an exemplary life, a model for the children and younger ones to follow, we should guide, nurture, teach and lead the next generation or our younger siblings towards a God-fearing life.

Finally, at work, there are always people working under us, under our authority. It may not be a whole nation like Joseph or Daniel, but big or small in numbers, - these are the children of God under your and my care.

A son's role is vital, for the Father wants continuity, and desires that His Masterplan be completed, as He has placed each of us in that responsible role as a 'son'. Jesus repeatedly asked Peter whether Peter loved Him, to which Peter answered, "Lord, you know that I do."

Jesus replied to Peter, "Feed my sheep." Being the good son and steward, our responsibility is to tend the flock and look after the sheep, i.e. all the children of God on earth, so that they will not go astray.

God has given us assets, talents, resources and funds at our disposal. Let us be good stewards of our life; it is still not too late to turn around, repent and change into a good steward, pleasing to our Father.

He is the LORD.

With good stewardship, comes responsibility, and with responsibility comes diligence. Hard work or working hard is essential for everyone.

Life is not easy, and man should not be lazy or take things easy in life. Even Adam before the fall had a major task to tend after the Garden of Eden, apart from ensuring 'multiplication of mankind', ruling the earth and dominating it, considering all the animals, creatures and birds of the air and fishes under Adam.

The Scriptures also rebuke the lazy or slothful individual. The Book of Proverbs has many verses telling all the detriment and end results of being lazy. The prodigal son was lazy, and wanted an easy life.

Thus, when the Master returned and found the steward doing all that evil, he rebuked him (Matthew 25:26) and said, "You wicked and lazy servant, you knew that I reap were I have not sown, and gather where I have not scattered seed." The steward was thrown into jail.

It pleases God, our Father when we work hard, and do our job well as good steward of our lives. Diligence is an essential part of the good steward's character.

Truly, indeed, hard work is never a flaw. Everyone appreciates a hard worker, and our Father is no different.

Jesus said, "My father is working even now". And Jesus, while He was on earth, ministering to the people, He worked very, very hard.

What is the evidence that Jesus worked very hard? Here are some of the examples, that come from the scriptures, clearly showing that He worked very hard.

He ministered to thousands and thousands as a group, until they were all hungry, needing food. That means that Jesus must have been teaching for at least 8 hours in a stretch, perhaps even more.

This story comes with the miracle of the five loaves and two fishes and again, repeated when he performed the miracle again before another crowd. His ability to feed the crowds became so 'famous', that He even said that many were coming to hear Him, not for the message but for the food, giving us a de javu feeling where we too seek a good meal, when we go for meetings.

Then again, there were times when he was tired and thirsty, so much that the disciples asked Him, what He was going to eat for food. One would not ask the teacher what food he was going to eat, if we have arrived from home, or from a meal. Jesus put work before food and comfort, and He said that 'His food' was to do the Father's work.

The scriptures also tell us that everyone in the region came for some meetings, and that everyone was healed; this means that some of the meetings went on and on, for hours throughout the night, possible finishing early in the morning. The scriptures also refer to the fact that it was Jesus alone, who was ministering during the few years of his ministry. None of his disciples took part in praying for the sick, meaning that it was one Person doing all the hard work.

Finally, at Gethsemane, when Jesus was praying, with His disciples, they fell asleep, suggesting that it was very tiring just to be a follower and disciple of Jesus, with crowds after crowds being ministered to, night after night.

Physically, mentally and emotionally, the few years with Jesus must have been equivalent to an apprentice attending a full-time course for a few years, day and night and night and day.

Can we then profess that we believe in Jesus, keep that belief locked up in a safe or cupboard, and get on with our normal daily life, seeking success in the world.

Diligence here, refers to hard work for the extension of the Kingdom of God, as much as it also refers to one being a responsible person on earth who works and does not shirk and laze around. Our Father expects us to work, to feed our family, and to feed the poor, the orphans, the widows, and to assist the foreigner.

The Bible refers to laziness, carelessness, or an easy-going attitude as being bad, because one will miss out on things of God, and the good example is that of the ten virgins, who were not prepared for the late arrival of the bridegroom.

During a season of strife or war, would one relax and watch television, even if it was working, while bombs are dropping around you? We are indeed in a time of war, spiritual war, and a battle in the air against the powers of darkness and principalities continue, hence much work to be done, even if the main work has already been done by our Lord on the Cross of Calvary.

The ant is quoted in the Bible as an example of a diligent worker. The ant is single minded in its purpose and duties.

Distractions is a good reason or excuse for every generation, and there are plenty of distractions for this generation.

Thus, being single minded, and putting the Kingdom of God first above all things, we have only one main purpose and that is to please the Father, and we can do so by being enlisted in His List of Workers and serve Him diligently.

All that we need to do is to offer ourselves before the Father and say, "Here I am, LORD."

God will find you your niche, your corner, your area of expertise and use you for the extension of His Kingdom.

To work, we have to rise up and get going, when the sun is shining, and go out into the harvest field, for the harvest is ripe and laborers are few.

And, there is no retirement age. Age is also secondary. Whether a teenager, a young adult, a mature adult, a middle-aged person, an elderly, or even a centurion, there is a ministry that awaits you.

Ministry begins where you are. Your home, your family, your neighborhood and your workplace are your 'Jerusalem'. Next, comes your Samaria, which is your city, your communities around you, strangers who pass by you, and your nation and the neighboring country.

When you have gone that far, then the rest of the world is at
your feet, especially in this modern day of travel.

Most of the time, you will be at your own 'Jerusalem', and
the few who are called to be evangelists, prophets and
apostles will travel further and reach out to the unreachable,
while the simple 'you and I' are the teachers and pastors,
situated right where we are.

There is no competition, and no need to jostle for positions,
and no need to pull brother or sister down from their
pedestals, for everyone has a platform, a place, even a pulpit
to minister from.

Whatever the denomination, whatever the theology, as long
as they preach Christ crucified and teachings are from the
Bible, welcome them and have fellowship with them. Build
the Kingdom, and not tear it down with strife. Strife and
conflict are negative activities that take up hours and hours of
wasted energy, while love, sharing and giving, whether the
word or resources is easy, friendly and builds relationships
and the Kingdom of God.

Ultimately, the work of our Father is to bring in all the sons
and daughters, making them good sons and daughters. To do
so, they must know that Father God loves them, and Father
God had specially sent His Son Jesus to die for all of
mankind, paying for the ransom of all the sins of the world.

All that one needs to do is to change our hearts, or repent
before our Father, say sorry, and call upon His Name, either
Father or LORD God, and acknowledge that He is our
Father, and that Jesus is His Son, and we immediately receive
our passport to Heaven.

In other words, our main and primary focus and work is to save souls, to bring them into the Kingdom of God. In so doing, we are co-laborers with the Holy Spirit of God, who does the conviction, and it will truly please our Father.

For what use is it if a man or woman gains the whole world and loses his or her soul?

Yes, success in the world is measured by achievements, position and wealth, none of which will entitle one entry into the Kingdom of God.

Entry into the Kingdom of God involves repentance, calling unto God, and receiving our Savior Jesus, who has facilitated our entry and will be there to open the Door into Heaven, because He is in fact 'The Door'.

He is the Passport, the Visa, the Password, and The Door into Heaven.

You and I, who already have that entry permit sealed, with our names written in the Book of Life, are His Ambassadors, and we have to share to others this wonderful news, so that when they hear, their open hearts will hearken to the word, and follow too.

How can they know if they do not hear, and how can they hear if we do not speak? God, through His Holy Spirit will hearken their hearts to receive the good news and when they call upon The LORD, they will be saved?

Begin today, by offering yourself as a co-laborer with the Holy Spirit by declaring, "Here I am Lord, at your service, ready to share the good news."

He will bring the harvest to you, or send you out to the harvest, for He is the LORD of the Harvest.

What are the benefits or fruits of good stewardship and diligence? The answer is simple and linked to obedience and trust, for as we are faithful in the little that is entrusted to us, more, if not all will be given to us.

In other words, God is constantly looking for laborers and workers in His Kingdom, and as we pass the test of good stewardship and are hardworking, he will appoint us to the next level of work. This is a promotion or breakthrough, as we are now empowered to do more, handle more and hence are now in a higher position of authority.

Luke 16:10-12 says, "He who is faithful in what is least is faithful also in much; and he who is unjust in what is least is unjust also in much. Therefore, if you have not been faithful in the unrighteous mammon, who will commit to your trust the true riches? And if you have not been faithful in what is another man's, who will give you what is your own?

So, our Father states this principle, which He applies every day, and that explains clearly why so many people remain poor, because they have not been faithful with whatever little God has given them.

So, the fruit of good stewardship and diligence, is God's abundance being poured into your life, because you can be trusted, having passed the test.

[[The opposite of the good steward is described in the parables. The bullying boss who beats up his servants,

while he enjoys his beer and merry making is not an uncommon scene these days. Cheap labor in the form of the foreign worker, (slavery in the past) is still ongoing in the world.

Human trafficking is no different than slavery, perhaps even worse. Mankind has been given the mandate to rule and subdue the world, to have dominion over birds, fishes and animals, but not on each other.

Good stewards are few and far in between. Even if you do not have workers or slaves under you, you are still responsible for your finances, assets and family members, and how you misuse your assets or look after your loved ones is a measure of your good stewardship.

The parable of the talents is clear. The one who received just one talent and kept in buried received a severe rebuke and punishment from the Master.

Your salvation is that `one talent'. Do you keep it to yourself, buried inside your heart without exposing it to the world to share the 'Good News'?

When we know that the Master is the One who provides for everything, and we are His stewards, we should then roll up our sleeves, and be a good steward, accountable to Him when He returns.]

The opposite of diligence is obvious. Being lazy or slothful is sometimes a trait of peaceful times. During war or strife, when danger is everywhere, there is no time for sleeping or being lazy, for being slow in fleeing, or being not diligent may mean death.

During hard times, one has to work hard to get water and food. When the ration truck arrives and you are not there with your container to collect the water, or not in line to pick up your food ration, you will miss it till the next round, which may be tomorrow.

In these easy times, all around the world, especially in the developed world, where the last war was over seven decades ago, obesity or an increasing waist line is evidence of some or more degrees of sloth.

Just after the Second World War in 1945, one would hardly see an 'obese' person, unless he or she was hiding in seclusion, with stacks and stacks of food that lasted the whole five or six years of strife.

Sleeping that extra hour, or resting that extra minute on the couch, being late for work, and postponing the responsibility till the next day is the opposite of diligence.

The plates are left in the sink, the beddings are in disarray (after all they will be messed up again tonight!), the clothes have not been washed for over a week, and living room, not just the garden and hedge are in a mess.

No wonder the saying, "Leave your comfort zone." Abraham, our father of nations was told to leave his comfort zone, and he literally stayed in tents all his life. The Israelites began to complain about life in the wilderness, because it was tough and hard work, compared to the 'comfort zone', though oppressed life in Egypt. A slave or a servant can have an easier life, as the master will provide food and shelter.

A free person, which you and I are now, has a choice – to work or to shirk.]

This author is just as guilty. We need to work while the sun shines, for a season will come when we have to run, in darkness or in pain, in sorrow or in tribulations, before the Son of Man returns again.]

EIGHT   Growing the Next Generation

The first commandment is clear. Multiply, and fill the earth, subdue it and have dominion over all the birds of the air, the fishes and the animals.

This may seem a small matter, but 'procreation' is a serious matter for Father God, so too for many parents of many traditions and cultures. Procreation ensures continuity. Kings and kingdoms for example for example look for an heir to the King, and the arrival of an heir or crown prince brings great joy to many nations.

God's plan is for many generations to go on, before the final picture, or ending.

One assumes that every couple or family will do the 'job' or play the role of ensuring the next generation to come. However, man and woman can get lazy, and conflict can interrupt plans, and change of attitude and inclination can also affect the process of procreation. In some large cities, perhaps only one in four families or less, are biologically functional, with man and wife.

Also, the busy couple would sometimes prefer to drop off to bed or enjoy a movie rather than engage in sex, if it was merely for procreation. For the animal kingdom, Almighty God has created biological ways for procreation to happen. For man and woman, it is the strong attraction between male and female, followed by a process of intimacy and copulation that brings great pleasure to both partners.

Thus, man and women, or mankind as a whole has fulfilled this commandment pretty well, literally spreading and filling up the whole earth, except for the extreme north and south, or the driest deserts and highest mountains. Man has moved and migrated from the beautiful Garden of Eden, to toil, subdue and develop the whole earth.

As an individual, everyone of us is a son or daughter. For the vast majority of us, we have an important role to move up as a father, mother, and then to the next level as grandfather and grandmother. For a few blessed ones, even a great grandparent role is attainable.

Considering that our forefathers before the great flood of Noah's time lived mostly a full millennium, they were alive for many more generations. This must clearly be for a purpose of overseeing the generations after you, to guide them on the right path before the LORD, long before the printed word, or recorded voice and video came into existence. Word of mouth, and teaching were passed down from generation to generation from forefathers down to the children and their children.

Thus, a God-fearing son or the good son has to raise the next generation in a God-fearing atmosphere, under a Godly guidance and teaching, in a loving environment and lift the next generation to a higher level.

At the right time and age, the good son or daughter does and should consider a partnership called 'marriage', a partnership that leads to off-springs and allows the next generation to rise up. Any other combination that does not allow for the multiplication and growth of the peoples of the nations, is not in line with God's plans. If men lose interest in women, and procreation becomes a chore that is neglected, the earth can become a depopulated planet. Just as a species can go extinct, mankind too can go extinct, if man and woman become non-fertile, or gets wiped out by disease or disaster, or when procreation and multiplication ceases.

God forbid that man will become extinct. No! The Lord Jesus will not return to an empty planet, even though God can raise stones to praise Himself.

The earth has to be full of men and women, eagerly awaiting His Glorious return, giving our Master and Lord a great and tumultuous welcome.

Men and women have to multiply, and the man must search for the partner, that the LORD provides, and the woman avail herself as an attractive virgin bride for her man.

Isaiah 34:16 is a great promise for all creation, belonging to the animal kingdom. The promise states: "No one will lack a mate."

This promise or word is for the owl, the jackal, the deer and all living creatures. Man, of course is not excluded, but with a difference – he or she has a choice, to choose his or her partner.

If one were to consider the critical decisions of one's life, a major one would be the search and choice of a life partner. It was so important for our father Abraham, our great patriarch that it was his great burden, considering what the LORD had promised him. The LORD had showed to him the skies and asked him to number the stars, and assured that Abraham would be a father of generations and their numbers could not be counted.

Thus, Abraham had to find a wife for his son Isaac. He directed and dispatched his chief servant for this crucial role, back to his homeland to find a partner for Isaac. This servant, whose name will remain unknown, was made to promise that he will diligently seek out Abraham's countrymen and seek a wife for his son.

God in his mighty provision, was with the servant, who had journeyed so far with his camels, arriving at his destination in good time. At the first instance, by the well where he stopped, beautiful Rebekah was there to water his camels. And he knew that the LORD had provided. Bowing head to the ground, he worshipped God then and there.

Remember too, the well-known story of how even the arrival of Isaac was a great challenge of faith. How could he at age 99 years perform the consummation to have a son, and how could his equally old wife bear a child at that age? But God had promised a year before that Sarah would bear a child the following year. And, God was faithful and His Promise came to pass.

Sarah could not help doubt, and laughed about it, but was rebuked. When the promise came to pass in the form of a beautiful son, Isaac, Abraham began an important journey of raising a son.

This is where the role of a parent comes in. In multiplication and in raising the next generation, our Father expects us to be responsible parents to raise the next generation in a correct, righteous and Godly way. It is not just about numbers, but also about quality. You, as a parent are to raise a prince or princess, after the order higher than Melchizedek, but after the order of Jesus Christ, a Christ-like follower.

This journey was not smooth, and Abraham had faltered before Isaac came. On the advice and nudging of his wife, Abraham went into Hagai, Sarah's maid and bore Ishmael. God, our Father did not rebuke or punish him, but told him clearly, that Ishmael was not the promise that He intended.

Sure enough, Isaac came, but when Isaac was a young lad, perhaps twelve or thirteen years of age, Abraham was given the ultimate test of his life. The LORD spoke to him clearly, and commanded him to take Isaac up to the mountain to sacrifice Isaac as an offering.

What a shocking directive! Abraham knew he heard clearly and he obeyed. He made urgent preparations, and told Isaac, but kept it a secret from Sarah, telling her that they had to go to the mountains, he and Isaac. He must have had a very, very heavy heart, literally interceding and praying over the night that God's will be done. He probably even did not pray against the LORD's directive, but just obeyed. How similar would this night be as that of our Lord Jesus, in Gethsemane!

He had obeyed to the very end, even to the point of tying up his son, laying him down on the altar, with the lad's understanding and permission, when at the very last second, with a knife raised up above him, that God would intervene.

Genesis 22.11-14 tells the story.

"Abraham, Abraham!" the Angel of the LORD had called out.

Abraham stopped and replied, "Here I am."

He had passed the test.

"Do not lay your hand on the lad, or do anything to him; for now, I know that you fear God, since you have not withheld your son, your only son, from Me."

Abraham looked up and saw a ram behind him, caught in a thicket. Abraham knew that "The LORD will provide."

Verses 16-18 are very powerful and the proclamation of blessings upon Abraham flows down to all mankind until today.

"By Myself, I have sworn, says the LORD, because you have done this thing, and have not withheld your son, your only son- blessing I will bless you, and multiplying I will multiply your descendants as the stars of the heaven and he sand which is on the seashore; and your descendants shall possess the gate of their enemies. In your seed all the nations of the earth shall be blessed, because you have obeyed My voice."

To fulfill that promise of God, man – i.e. you and me, have to fulfill that crucial role, to marry, bear children and raise them up in a God-fearing way.

The good son or daughter, thus must or should become a father or a mother. God will not only find you a good and right partner, but God will open the womb of your wife, or your womb (dear wife) to bear a child, and the child will be blessed as a descendant of Abraham, one among the stars and the sands that God has promised.

The journey of the good son or daughter takes a new dimension, when the good son or daughter becomes the good parent, a role that is very crucial too. Many, including this author will testify that there is great faithfulness in our Father (the hymn – 'Great is thy faithfulness comes to mind), when we see the blessings that so clearly go on to the next generation, often another level, a higher level and a special level too.

Your child, son or daughter grows up being known as your son or daughter, but before long, the community or people whether in church or outside will soon know him or her, on his or her own right, and you then become known as your child's parent! The next generation has arrived, and will rightfully overtake you and rise up to take a higher role.

Rejoice for God has been faithful, to raise the next generation to a higher level then you, even if you call that fame or name.

This good son has to play the role of being a good father, or parent. In other words, the role of a good son continues by being the good father, the good grandfather and the good great grandfather.

In summary, the good father must provide, lead, care, guide, protect, nurture, love, bless, explain, show by example, teach, and correct his or her child, son or daughter in raising up a Godly child.

Good Godly parenting would be the content of another book or title.

What is the benefit of empowering the next generation, through biological means or adoption? Because you endeavor to raise a righteous generation, holy before God, the obvious fruit of it is a new generation, which is blessed, holy and righteous before God.

Generations and generations after you will be blessed as they carry the Name of the LORD, and live the life of godliness for the LORD.

There have been documentations that some family lines are filled with murderers, rapists, thieves, convicts and the like, while another is blessed with professionals, congressmen, leaders, senators, judges, ministers and successful businessmen.

There may be many factors resulting in such a phenomenon, but clearly one of them, is the generation before us, whether they had put the input of prayer and effort to raise a strong and righteous generation before God.

[The opposite of multiplying and growing the next generation is not nurturing the next generation. It is not necessarily being single or not being a parent, as one can still bless and multiply the next generation, even as a single bachelor, as both of the greatest teachers were, the Lord and Paul.

Any action that is opposite of being 'Pro Life" or any action that works against nurturing godliness in the young, or any scientific research and attempt to create clones and prototypes of the human form that is different from the original Adam and Eve would trigger an opposition if not wrath from the LORD.

Obviously too, any attempt or act to terminate life, apart from valid medical reasons would make the womb a tomb.

Few realize the tragedy of the 'womb of life becoming a tomb of death' when termination of life is deliberately done whether at four weeks or more.

Apart from that, if one bears children and lets them run loose unprotected and exposed to the evil of the world, without guidance, nurturing, teaching and leading, we risk them becoming an ungodly generation.

One wonders too why a godly king can beget an ungodly king, yet we see it a lot at the succession during the time of the kings and prophets.

When one is not married, or if the marriage for some reason has not produced offspring, one can still adopt 'children', whether legally or unofficially, to guide them on.

One can also be a 'father', 'mother' or God-parent to many children, whether as a guardian, teacher, or a friend. Everyone can and should contribute towards the next generation, by raising up children either biologically or through adoption, and through one's contact and interaction with the next generation.

Hence, having children and saying, "That's it – I have provided food, shelter and education for you all. My responsibility ends there" is insufficient and incorrect.

As parents and guardians, our input and role go beyond that. We need to guide, teach, lead and discipline our next generation, never spoiling them nor abusing them, so that there will be no Cains or Esaus.]

NINE   Righteousness

Righteousness is a defining characteristic or quality that this author believes is synonymous with God, and reflects the purity and holiness of His Majesty.

This author's own definition would be that if the opposite of right is wrong, and there is a scale reflecting the range, then righteousness or being righteous is on the extreme and ultimate end of being right, and only God is in that position.

One can almost be certain that unless one is righteous, one cannot expect to enter God's Presence, i.e. the Holy of holies, and being clothed with the garment of holiness. The Kingdom of God in Heaven receives only the righteous, eliminating all who fall short of that standard, a very high one indeed.

For that reason, in the days before the first coming of the Messiah, the priest could not enter the most holy and central part of the temple without undergoing a process of cleansing. And this special entry into God's Holy Presence was allowed only once a year.

With the coming of Jesus, the Messiah, all our sins have been cleansed and washed away by the blood shed in Calvary, for He is the Lamb of God, whose Blood is the redemption of the sins of mankind. We are thus now clothed with the garment of holiness, enabling us to enter the Holy of Holies freely, entering His Presence freely.

Yet, righteousness, holiness, godliness or goodness may sound a cliché, if not a 'provocative' word for many people, both the non-Christian and even some believers, whether Bible believing or Pentecostal, charismatic tongue-speaking. Oddly too, few Christians declare that 'we are the righteousness of God in Christ', though it is the truth, and this truth sets us free.

One definition in the internet defines 'righteousness' as the quality of being morally right and justifiable, giving it synonyms of goodness, virtue, uprightness, decency, integrity, worthiness, rectitude, probity, morality, ethicalness, high-mindedness, justice, honesty, honor, innocence, blamelessness, guiltlessness, irreproachability, sinlessness, saintliness, purity, nobility, noble-mindedness, piety, and piousness.

God is God and has no sin, and God's criteria for entry into His Kingdom is that anyone who enters is 'free of sin', and this has been made possible by the 'Lamb of God' sacrificed on the Cross of Calvary for all of mankind.

When God sees us, cleansed and pure, and righteous before Him, He is pleased.

The word 'righteousness' appears in the Bible (NKJV) 296 times, many of it in the Old Testament. Righteousness comes from the LORD, and is our protection as the breast plate of our armor.

Isaiah 59:17, "For He put on righteousness as a breastplate." (also, in Ephesians 6:14)

One may rudely sneer or doubt when a friend declares that he or she intends to lead a life of righteousness and godliness. Are we not all supposed to do so?

A common and acceptable stance or posture is that we are all are sinners, saved by grace, and no one is perfect; so why do we overemphasize on stress on being 'perfect' or being good in the eyes of God, for it is He who makes us clean, pure and perfect.

They say: "Rather than struggle to be perfect, why not let go and let God cleanse us of our sins, and our imperfections.

God is a loving God, not one who will destroy the sinner so easily, as He has given us a Son and Savior Jesus. This realization will take us away from the stress and struggle to be righteous, because no matter how hard we try, we will fail or be flawed."

The doctrine that our salvation is not by our works and deeds but by the grace or gift from God holds true as the pillar of the Christian faith. Why then should we struggle to be righteous and maintain our righteousness?

This is a paradox for some who try very hard, even to do penance, when all our efforts cannot earn or win our salvation. The work has already been done.

Why then are we so prone to sin, even as a believer in Christ, as Paul himself asserts too? Paul says, paraphrased, "What I desire to do, I do not, and fail to do, but what I do not wish to do, I do!"

This author believes that the answer is in 'Grace' and 'Grace' again, for the first 'Grace' is the completed work of Jesus on the Cross, and that 'Grace' is the 'Lamb of God', who was slain for our redemption, thus enabling us to enter God's Presence.

The second or continuing 'Grace' is the same as the first 'Grace' because 'Grace' is still there for us to enable us to 'sin no more', but live in the abundance of love and life from Christ Jesus, our Savior. This is an effortless thing, when we surrender, submit and allow God to work the new creation in us.

For that reason, John 15:5 says, "apart from Jesus, we can do nothing!", for we are the branches, and Jesus is the Vine, and God the Father is the Vinedresser.

This is the Truth and the Truth will and should set you and I free.

We are already saved, and this grace or ongoing strength from God will enable us to live a holy and righteous life, by His strength, not ours even daily! For that reason, it is wrong to say that, "From now on, I will live a life of holiness and righteousness", if we do not qualify with the phrase, "by the Grace of God." For on our own strength, we will fail, but with God's strength and grace, we will triumph over sin and evil and be righteous before God.

It is therefore correct to press on and pursue living a righteous life, and grasp it as a virtue that God desires, and above all, a virtue from God, not something achieved with our own strength. Almost everything is given through grace, and all we need to do is receive it with faith.

Firstly, we know that 'Salvation', our salvation is through grace, not by our works or efforts, but given to us for free, because of the redemptive and finished work of Jesus on the Cross of Calvary, once and for all.

Secondly, our righteousness or holiness is through no small or big effort of us, but we are now clothed with garments of holiness and praise, enabling us to enter God, our Father's Presence.

Thirdly, our strength, ability and empowerment are from God, for apart from Him, we can do nothing. (John 15:5)

Therefore, we should not take righteousness, godliness, holiness and goodness lightly, and live a sinful life recklessly. Rather, we should endeavor to understand our (man's) weakness and failings and know that we stand righteous before God, by His grace i.e. that we have been made perfect before God by the Blood of the Lamb.

This author being Pentecostal, charismatic and tongue-speaking is fully committed to the doctrine of baptism of the Holy Spirit, and holds a firm belief that everyone should seek this baptism, because it is from God.

The Bible does say that "not all will speak in tongues", and not all gifts of the Holy Spirit will be given to all believers (indirectly in Corinthians); yet if one seeks it, one will receive it, for sure.

Also, the vast majority, if not all the authors of the Bible, are 'tongue' speaking. Clearly, while being baptized in the Holy Spirit, being filled with the Holy Spirit, or 'speaking in tongues' is a good and awesome thing, it does not equal to attaining righteousness or godliness.

God hates sin, and righteousness is clearly opposite of sin, for sin leads to death and righteousness will earn us eternal life.

Righteousness is without doubt an important criterion that is pleasing to the LORD, because our LORD is holy and righteous. Righteousness is God, and God is our Father. He does not lie; He does not cheat; He does not steal; He does not do evil. He is Good, all the time.

God is a good and loving God all the time, and He wants to bless His beloved children, His sons and His daughters. Sin and evil stands in the way to all these blessings, whereas righteousness opens the door for blessings and love freely.

Righteousness may be almost synonymous with holiness, godliness, goodness and purity, though there may be subtle differences. Again, each of these characteristics or descriptions of a believer can sound extreme and very high as a standard. Yet, our God is a righteous God, and no matter what definition and explanation we may have to describe righteousness, perhaps the best is that our God is a righteous God, and righteousness is being right, correct and perfect in all aspects, before a righteous God.

Psalm 11:7, "For the LORD is righteous, He loves righteousness; His countenance beholds the upright.

We should therefore emulate our Savior Jesus, for He is the true Son of righteousness, and we too are sons and daughters of righteousness.

However, we can definitely say that God is righteous, God is pure, God is holy and God is good, for God is God. Is not man made with the image and likeness (character) of God? Is not a baby born pure, innocent and holy before 'corruption and depravity' sets in.

Mankind has been saved ever so often because of one such good man or woman. There was Enoch who walked with God after the fall, and it pleased God. There was Noah, who was blameless before God. Mankind was and is saved from destruction by the great flood, because of him. Then there was father Abraham who was counted as righteous before God. For through Father Abraham, generations after generations of the Jewish people, and gentiles now are made righteous too, as we are grafted into the Jewish link, through Abraham. Then there was Esther who stood in the gap for the people of Israel, risking her life before the King, when she approached Him, without appointment, hence successfully petitioning and saving the Jewish race from being wiped out. Then there was Zechariah, from whom a front runner for Jesus was born – John the Baptist. And of course, there is the Good Son, the Son of God who was and is pure and is the spotless Lamb of God, who died as a ransom for all the sins of mankind.

It is true that all men have sinned and that the wages of sin is death; for that reason, Jesus came to stand in for us, so that we can be made blameless and righteous before the Throne of God.

It is because the original purpose of our salvation is so that we are made righteous, and hence accepted by God, our Father, who is a Holy and Righteous God. When we are saved by the grace of God, we are made holy and righteous before God, and granted His Holy garment over us, cleansed by the Blood of the Lamb.

Psalm 23 says that He leads us in the paths of righteousness, and Psalm 24:5 says "he shall receive blessing from the LORD, and righteousness from the God of his salvation."

Righteousness and holiness are often taken for granted by many charismatics and tongue-speaking, for it is so easy and convenient to come before our Father and ask freely from Him. We are so delighted to have full access to a loving God, and thus can often enter His Presence despite living a tainted and contaminated life, knowing that He is a gracious and merciful God. But, as Paul says, we do not continue to sin because of grace, and for sure those who choose that path of deliberately sinning and sinning again and again, will be revealed, and in the end fall in shame.

Many devoted and committed believers from many Orthodox, Catholic, Protestant and evangelical denominations emphasize the need to be God-fearing and law abiding as believers. So-called 'born again' believers in contrast, may take offence when we are told to be righteous and holy, because the teaching and Word is clear, that we are already made righteous by the grace of God. It is true that we are already so, for we are righteous with the Christ in us. The troubling question is why do so many still carelessly and recklessly continuing to live in sin? Grace does not give one a license to sin, as Paul says!

Romans 6:1, "What shall we say then? Shall we continue in sin that grace may abound?" He continued with the answer in the next verse, "Certainly not!"

Romans 10:4 says, "For Christ is the end of the law for righteousness to everyone who believes."

For that reason, we should remain righteousness, rather than abuse it or take it for granted. Every believer should live a God-fearing, law abiding life, with holiness and righteousness being central in their walk before God, no matter what our denomination or doctrinal belief is, as long as they believe that Jesus is the Son of God, and Savior of the world.

It is perfectly all right to take the law seriously, watch our steps cautiously, and even watch each other's steps closely, so that we do not slip from our exalted God given position, as sons of God, as holy priests, and fall into temptation.

We should not end up being like the Pharisees in spending so much energy doing so, and hence condemning each other because of each other's shortcomings, but rather, we should receive grace and live in it effortlessly. For the Word of God says that unless our righteousness exceeds that of the Pharisees, we will not see God.

Jesus himself said, "For I say to you, that unless your righteousness exceeds the righteousness of the scribes and Pharisees, you will by no means enter the kingdom of heaven.

Thus, righteousness and holiness should be a natural part of us, as we desire to live a life pleasing to God, one that is renewed, an unblemished life, speck-less or spotless before God. And, it is through grace that we are made righteous before God.

The very moment we talk of being speckled-free and blemish free on our own strength, we will run into problems of trying to be perfect before God, and knowing that only God is perfect.

Remember that God saw Noah, and Zechariah and found them blameless, or blemish free. Thus, it is not about us focusing on being perfect, but joyously being holy and righteous before God, as a part of our walk with God, because He is a Holy and Righteous God, and we love to please Him, follow Him and walk with Him, alongside Him.

Since we know what is right and wrong, do we not turn away from sin and unrighteous living, for God has not only made us righteous, but given us the strength to continue to live in righteousness, with the Holy Spirit in us, guiding and teaching us.

1 John 2:1 says, "My little children, these things I write to you, so that you may not sin. And if anyone sins, we have an Advocate with the Father, Jesus Christ the righteous."

How can we claim to be righteous, if we are into pornography, lusting after our own flesh, coarse and vulgar in our words, and doing deeds which are evil? Can we then, walk side by side with our LORD? Thus, when the heart is right before God, and when we decide to follow Him, we will set ourselves apart for Him, and be holy and righteous.

How does the good son deal with temptation, with sex, with greed, with power and with riches? Is it possible? Is it attainable, when we see so many men of God falling in sin?

Whose fault is it? Were they weak, or is it the accuser and tempter to be blamed?

For sure, the tempter is waiting around the corner to assist you, if you are not careful, if you give the slightest opportunity or opening for the enemy to come in. Caution, precaution, preparation and perseverance, apart from sacrifice are what champions need, to reach their target, and remain as champions. Why should it be made easy and less different for a man or woman of God? For that reason, we pray the Lord's Prayer that we will not be tempted, but delivered from evil.

It does require wisdom, apart from effort, caution, precaution, preparations and perseverance to live a holy and righteous life, though it is by the Grace of God. For example, if you, as a man of God, are going out to meet a beautiful lady alone, it is natural for you to be tempted, and if you are also a handsome young man, it is a situation that either can fall for the lady can also be tempted. Or if you are travelling together with a working partner, you and the same lady, an office mate, and away from home, staying in the same hotel, - is that not putting both parties at a very high risk?

What then is the precaution? You set your heart and mind right, not to allow your thoughts to drift towards sin. Watch your words, guard your eyes, watch your language and say 'No!' long before the risk becomes sin. Nip it in the bud.

By preparing yourself, you can become like Joseph, who ran away from sin. For the man, think of Joseph, and prepare yourself to run away, when you enter any premise alone to find a beautiful young lady, skimpily dressed inside your apartment.

For the young, or even older lady, be ready not to accept advances and to rebut them early. A simple, "No, I am married" should put many off, and if necessary, follow through with a firm: "I said 'No!'"; and if the guy still persists, slam him with a strong rebuke, "Please leave now, or I will report you!"

Likewise, with pornography, control your finger with a clear direction, "No to pornography." The Holy Spirit will also guide you when you give Him the full permission. You will hear Him speak to you, and say words like, "Stop", "No", or "well done", when you resist and obey.

Caution, preparation, precaution, and a determined strong will, will make a holy and righteous life walkable and doable. Do we not do it all the time? If you do not drink whisky, and you are offered a drink, will you drink from it, or politely say no? Should you let someone force something that you do not want down your throat? Therefore, it is within your power, ability and strength to say "No" to sin, and say "Yes" to righteousness.

When you succeed time and time again, you will find that the righteous and holy walk is a part of your life, and people will recognize that and see the glory of God in your life.

The LORD's prayer is clear, to pray that we are not led into temptation, and are delivered from evil.

God will give us the strength to be strong and battle against the desires and lust of the flesh, so that we can focus on Godly things, and not be distracted by fleshly desires.

Righteousness is for our own good, as the teaching and doctrine in Matthew 6:33 declares: "Seek first the kingdom of God and His righteousness, and all these things shall be added to you."

We often quote the first part i.e. the kingdom of God, and forget or omit the second. God desires us to seek His righteousness, so that we can be righteous too, like God.

What's so great about being holy and righteous – the critic will say! Well, we know that the fervent prayer of a righteous man will avail much. That is very powerful a truth, that such a person's prayers work and will be answered.

James 5:16, "The effective, fervent prayer of a righteous man avails much." What more reason do we need to be right and righteous in the eyes of God?

[The opposite of righteousness is sinfulness, in whatever form or amount.

The critics of righteousness will thus condemn the extreme of a pharisaical approach or the Amish way that denies one of a good life, through strictly follow the law, punishing those who have done wrong, and avoiding the pleasures of life. This is incorrect path towards righteousness, as it is actually more a form of religiousness.

All have sinned and literally, no one can try to be righteous on one's own ability or steam.

Then, we have the other extreme, knowing that God is a good and gracious God, and hence falling in sin is a small matter, for He will forgive. This is the other 'dangerous' extreme of one who abuses the 'Grace of God' and sins freely, entering promiscuity, sexual sins, and all forms of

deceits and evil that is in man, crossing over the line by miles, and may even fall out of grace!

God, our Father is not deceived or fooled or foiled by our misdeeds. He looks at the heart - a good heart, one after God's heart. One cannot lead a sinful life of evil, drunkenness, sexual immorality, carefreeness on weekdays, and then preach a Godly God-fearing message on weekends, for long. He cannot get away from leading an unrighteous, unrepentant life for long, without seeing the ground under him giving way. You and I cannot deceive God.]

TEN   Generous Giving

Giving, or generous giving and sharing of one's wealth and resources is a central part of Christian life. It is in fact, one of the signs or evidence of Christian love and Christian living.

It begins with the truth and knowledge that all things come from God, and it is He who supplies all our needs. Thus, giving back a portion, a tenth in Levitical Law, is among the statutes in the Old Testament, though not directly listed in the Ten Commandments. Tithing is only a part of giving, as there are other forms of offerings, and sacrifice described in the Old Testament.

Tithing or given a tenth of your earnings, or what you have earned or your income, continues to be a teaching, and a healthy practice for the believer, under the New Testament.

Abraham was the first to give a tenth to Melchizedek, after he had blessed and prayed for Abraham, following his deliverance from his enemies.

Genesis 14:20, "And he gave him a tithe (a tenth) of all."
Note that the Bible says, a tenth of all that Abraham
possessed.

This was followed by Jacob, who pledged or vowed that he
would give a tenth of what he received from the LORD.

Genesis 28:22, "And this stone which I have set as a pillar
shall be God's house, and all that You give me I will surely
give a tenth to You."

Deuteronomy 12:6 describes burnt offerings, sacrifices,
tithes, heave offerings, vowed offerings and freewill
offerings, and ultimately the firstborn of one's herds, flocks,
(and one's firstborn male), as all the various offerings to the
LORD.

When this author was expecting his firstborn male child, the
LORD spoke and said clearly, "This child is mine, your
firstborn son; give him to Me." Then and then, the son was
given to the LORD. Giving is more than just dedication.
Giving is giving. Nevertheless, have we forgotten that we are
now our own, for all of us have been bought for a price, by
His life on the Cross.

1 Corinthians 6:19,20 "Or do you not know that your body is
the temple of the Holy Spirit who is in you, whom you have
from God, and you are not your own. For you were bought at
a price; therefore, glorify God in your body."

If we take the clock and move the dial from 12, at six
minutes past 12, the hand or dial would represent a tenth of
an hour, or a tithe. In one of this author's sermon on giving,
the Holy Spirit reminded me that the giver who tithes right
on the dot of a tenth, though a good and law-abiding believer,
is in fact a 'Stingy Christian'. He or she is a miser, counting

just exactly how much 'tax' he or she has to return to God, in the form of a tithe.

With love and maturity, the believer should learn to give more than a tenth, crossing over the six minutes mark, even nearly to the point of giving away half of his assets. That is what one should call a 'Generous Giver', sharing more and more of his or her blessings, all of which comes from God.

After all, the Bible is clear that when we give to the poor, we lend to God, and God is a prompt payer to those He owes!

Proverbs 19:17 says, "He who has pity on the poor lends to the LORD. And He will pay back what he has given."

Moving the hand of the clock from 6 minutes towards 30 is an exciting journey that this author experienced; giving can initially be 'painful', but as one learns generosity, and when one understands the Heart of our Father, and keeps giving and giving, a breakthrough takes place and giving becomes a joyful and natural exercise.

Almost every father out there would happily give half of all they have to their beloved, often the wife and children. They slog a life time, and happily give away half of all that they have to their beloved.

King Herod offered that to his daughter, when he was so pleased with her dancing, offering half of his kingdom to her.

Giving half, when the dial touches 30, is in this author's opinion, a "Loving Giver", and natural thing to do, when one gives to one's family and beloved.

The challenge or test is to give away half to charity or others, and many rich philanthropists have done so. Bill Gates and his wife, are perhaps one of the largest givers in the world, and give away a lot to various charities and projects, making his personal position dip from the richest man in the world, to lower from time to time. One may recall many billionaires, who are generous givers, who say, "I do not need so much money for myself; that's why I donate to charity."

Once one has touched the 30 dial, there is no stopping the giver. The challenge comes when one crosses over beyond 30, as now there is a sacrifice involved. Instead of buying a huge luxurious bungalow, your funds only allow a comfortable big bungalow. You have made the sacrifice to reduce your available assets when you continue to give beyond 50% of your life time assets or savings.

This author calls it the "Sacrificial Giver", when you feel the pinch, if not pain, because it now involves a sacrifice in your own life.

When does giving stop? At what point is giving considered excellent? The answer is that, it does not stop at 10% (the stingy Christian), nor 25% (the generous Christian), nor 50% (the loving Christian, who shares), or the 75% giver, who is indeed a sacrificial Christian.

The ultimate test is the giver who gives all, or the 'Total Giver'.

Jesus relates the story of a rich man who was pleased to tell the Lord that he had complied with everything that the law had required of him. He asked the million-dollar question to Jesus Himself, "What should I do now?"

Quoting Matthew 19:21,22, Jesus said to him, "If you to be perfect, go, sell what you have and give to the poor, and you will have treasure in heaven; and come, follow Me."

"But when the young man heard that saying, he went away sorrowful, for he had great possessions."

For a long time, this author had pity or sympathy for the rich man, that he was given the challenge to give all away. While preparing for a recent sermon, the revelation came and hit me like a rock.

Jesus, our Master obviously is right. For, if the man is seeking God, and all that is from God, the answer was right in front of him – Jesus Himself. If he was to follow Jesus, he had everything, and he needed nothing, hence rightfully should give away all and put his life in God's Hand, by following Jesus.

The disciples and followers were all well fed and fine, as long as they followed Jesus. Have we considered what happened to their needs, when Jesus ascended to Heaven?

The story of the poor lady who gave 'two mites', which was all that she had is often preached in church. The Lord Jesus said, that this lady had given more than the whole congregation combined in her giving, because she gave all that she had. She was a total and sacrificial giver, as she had just given away her lunch and her dinner for the day.

In the days of past, and even in this modern day, there are many who would give away everything, their inheritance, their cushy job, their savings, to enter a monastery or nunnery.

Thus, generous giving is a reflection of God's Heart in you and I. For sure, it makes our Father happy, and the reverse is true. Our Father is displeased to see the 'poor' giver, and even angry and upset, when the poor cry to Him in their hunger and misery, because the rich around them do not care or love enough to give and feed the poor.

Generous giving is a process. Start small and simple. Give 10 dollars or whatever your equivalent in denomination is. You can progress in multiples, doubling or adding a zero each time you progress in your life. From 10, rise up to 100 dollars, and soon you will find it a joy to give 1000, and when you are blessed richly, 10,000 and 100,000 will be your next challenge, before you progress to 1 million or more.

Never say that you will start to give when you are as rich as Bill Gates. The teaching in Luke 16:10-12 is very clear. You need to be faithful with a little, before you can hope to see the millions.

Luke 16:11,12 "Therefore if you have not been faithful in the unrighteous mammon, who will commit to your trust the true riches? And if you have not been faithful in what is another man's, who will give you what is your own?"

No wonder Jesus said that one can only worship either God or mammon.

Matthew 6:24, "No can serve two masters; for either he will hate the one and love the other, or else he will be loyal to the one and despise the other; You cannot serve God and mammon."

As Jesus said to the rich man, it is a matter of getting detached and attached. Detach yourself from the things of the world, material things and riches, and get attached to God, God's word, prayer and worship, and you will be on the right track.

The heart or art to give begins when you understand our Father's Heart, and His love for you and I, and for all of His creation.

God has blessed you with plenty and abundance; share your blessings, and return the first fruits of your blessings to God, through giving.

[The opposite of being a generous giver is one who unselfishly hoards his wealth, or even in his lack, does not give to the poor.

When examined closely, almost every believer is guilty of not being generous in giving. Equally bad are all the churches, who are literally guilty of hoarding the tithes, and using it for structural 'church building' and church expansion or renovation, when the poor come in week after week, without being fed.

Generous giving is a rare practice in church and in the believer, even the born-again Spirit filled believer, in this author's opinion. The reasons for it being selfishness, greed and love of money and riches.

This is very sad but true.

ELEVEN   Love & Worship our Father

The first and foremost commandment, that sums up all the ten commandments, is to love our Father in Heaven.

Jesus said, in Matthew 22:37 & 38, "You shall love the LORD your God, with all your heart, with all your soul, and with all your mind. This is the first and great commandment."

It is recorded again in Mark's Gospel, Chapter 12, verse 20, "And you shall love the LORD your God with all your heart, with all your soul, with all your mind, and with all your strength.' This is the first commandment.

It has been positioned at No.11, not because it is that low in importance, but as guided by the Holy Spirit, it is placed after the rest, in God's gracious eyes.

There is supporting scriptures where our Father gives emphasis to us to do the right things for our own good. Certainly, before you can even love our Father, we need to know Him, hence the first step being to 'acknowledge Father' and to call Him. Many millions and millions of people on planet earth have never called our Father even once. And, if at all they have mentioned His Name, it is in vain, either as a swear word or even a curse.

Next, before we can have a relationship, we need to set right our hearts, and our Father so desires that we are grateful people, offering thanks and thanksgiving always. Furthermore, at His first early encounter with the people He chose, as a nation of His choice, a nation to guide and lead in a Godly way, under His Fatherly guidance, He gave the Ten Commandments.

And the Ten Commandments, which is the Law, was personally written by God's fingers, not once but twice on sacred Tablets, defining His rules for His people, which include all the peoples of the world. Although, these rules are never to be broken, The LORD allowed grace and mercy to forgive the rule-breakers. The Law remains.

Thus, obedience to God's Laws followed by 'kindness and mercy' and the others have been listed ahead of this 11th expectation of our Father. Our Father expects us to acknowledge Him with thanksgiving, draw near to Him, and be obedient, diligent, kind, generous and righteous, multiplying for the next generation and raising them up with responsibility, even before He expects us to love and worship Him.

What is the evidence? The WORD of God is very strong on this. Our Father prefers obedience than our sacrifice. In other words, it is no point if we bow before Him and declare our love and worship, when we fail in the first ten, because it provokes God, as He has often said, that He is sick of the offerings of bulls and rams, and does not want anymore of that, from those who sin against Him, or His people.

Nevertheless, love remains the first and greatest of all commandments, and love is the central attribute of our God. Our Father is love, and He desires His children, all of whom are made in His Image to love Him in return. The emphasis is very strong – to love The LORD, with all our heart, all our might, all our soul, all our mind, and all our energy, literally everything is us.

Should there be any question by any critic or doubters as to why we need to love God?

In reality, everything in us is from God (John Chapter 1), and apart from Him, we can do nothing (John 15:5), and literally every cell, organ, organ system in our body reflects God's intelligence, God's perfection, God's organization for those whose eyes are opened to see the glory of God (not nature) in the human body, mind and soul.

If the LORD is our Maker, and our survival depends totally on Him, it is only natural, rational and sensible that this organ structure called man should honor, glorify and love God, The LORD GOD, all the days of our life.

The next natural question that crops up to all believers, is how?

My son-in-law David Ng received a revelation from the LORD that God never expects from us anything that He has not Himself done to us or for us; thus, whatever God desires us to do for Him or to Him, He has already done the same to us and for us. And everything that the LORD does for us is good, and it is always for our own good, when He directs us to do according to His wishes.

It was God who first loved us, and gave His only begotten Son to die for us on the Cross, and that His love for us is so overwhelming, so great, so deep and so wide, that He desires the same for us, towards Him.

This deep love that God our Father has for us, individually and as a race, i.e. human beings, for the whole of mankind is the main awesome attraction between man and God.

Because, God our Father is so deeply in love with you and I, that He desires that all should come to repentance and that none should perish. For that reason, our Father rejoices when every soul is saved in the Kingdom of God.

Even though the wages of sin is death, God gave us His Son to pay the ransom and price to set us free.

Once a deep realization of what God has done for us sinks in deep into our hearts, the love and passion for our LORD rises up and we seek from the LORD what we should do for Him.

How then should we love our LORD, with all our heart, all our mind, all our strength and all our soul.

Firstly, it begins with acknowledging Him as our LORD and Father, followed by thanksgiving and a life that is pleasing to

Him, one with obedience, diligences, intimacy, kind, generous, caring, apart from playing our responsibility to ourselves, family and society. Next, is to respond to God, our Father to do His Will and serve Him.

A Master and owner has a mission and purpose. God, our Father's main mission is to save the souls of mankind, and His wish is that none should perish.

2 Peter 3.9 states very clearly, "The Lord is not slack concerning His promise, as some count slackness, but is longsuffering toward us, not willing that any should perish but that all should come to repentance."

We know that the Lord Jesus has already come, and paid the price of our ransom by His death and sacrifice on the Cross. And this is the Good News that Salvation comes through Jesus Christ, that he who calls upon the Name of the Lord will be saved.

His desire thus is that we do the work as His ambassador, as His spokesperson, to be "fishers of men and women". We do so by sharing the Good News, telling the world that Jesus is the Savior of the World, and all things came from Him and when we believe in Him, we will be born again into the Kingdom of God.

In Peter's case, Jesus asked him three times, if he loved the LORD. It was to feed the sheep, to guide and teach them in the Word and Law.

In conclusion, to love the LORD, we ought to acknowledge Him, be grateful, draw close to Him, know His Word and obey His commandments, and serve Him faithfully, diligently and be the good steward until He comes.

As His ambassador, we are to promote and tell the world about Jesus, as any ambassador promotes his or her country or product. We are to carry His light, shine for Him, and share the Gospel or 'Good News' about our Savior Jesus.

How do we do so? With all our might, all our mind, all our heart and all our soul!

Human nature is such that it is natural for you and I to love the rich, the famous, the powerful and the handsome and beautiful. We can literally admire, rush to meet, and kiss the richest man in the world, the most famous actor or entertainer, Mr Universe or Miss Universe, but will keep a distance from the poor wretched, smelly, sick, worm-infested beggar outside our gates begging for the day.

Why then is it so difficult to love the LORD our Father, when our Father and His Son are indeed the wealthiest of the wealthiest, being the owner of all that is on earth and the Universe, the most powerful among the powerful, the King of kings, and our Father, as seen in His Son Jesus is not just the most famous, but the most beautiful and handsome of all that have ever existed in Heaven and earth.

That is why, truly, we should bow down before Him, adore Him and worship Him all the days of our life.

God our Father is Majesty, the King Who sits upon the Throne. Worship and praise are naturally due to Him, as an act of our deep love for Him.

Any good son or daughter will automatically come before the Father in obeisance, and bow down to worship God, our Father.

In traditional Eastern culture, the 'good son' is the filial son, who continues to worship the ancestors in the form of an altar, where the image is placed i.e. a photograph, with offerings including food place on regular intervals, as a sign of being a 'good son.' Many parents, who subscribe to this faith called 'Taoism', therefore always look towards a loyal and filial son to 'pray for them' after their death. Among some of the practices, there are burnt offering of 'paper money' even strangely called "Hell Bank notes" and other luxurious items like paper car, paper handphones and paper houses or palaces, which are not cheap. Purchase of some of these paper items can run to several thousands of dollars. This example is just to explain how such a concept of worship can be entrenched even in a religion.

In Old Testament practice, worship and offerings include burnt offerings of unblemished animal and bird species.

If one searches the scripture for the word 'worship', invariably on many occasions, it refers to worship and bowed down, head to the ground.

Bowing down is an act of respect, followed very closely in the Japanese culture, when they greet each other. Bowing down to deities, idols and other gods is also a common practice, and one particular faith imposes the bowing down head to the ground as a form of prayer and worship, till we see scars on their foreheads. Many believers have perhaps never even once bowed down with head touching the ground to worship the Father, our LORD GOD.

You need to do so, whenever you worship the LORD GOD, for true worship is bowing down with head to the ground.

Since Grace through Jesus Christ came, we have become God's friends, and enjoy a close relationship, on a first name basis! We can enter the holy of Holies and call upon Him freely, with full access to our LORD.

Rites and rituals are literally non-existent for the born-again believer, with even festivals and ceremonies being not necessary, except perhaps the baptism in water by full emersion.

Worship also now takes more than just bowing down with head to the ground. Singing songs of praise is worship. Lifting our hands, clapping, praying out loud and in tongues is also worship. Playing instruments of music, e.g. Psalm 150 is definitely also instrumenting of praise and worship. Dancing before the LORD can also be worship. Likewise, generous giving is also worship and praise.

Nevertheless, we know many cases, including the experiences of the saints, that in the holy and awesome presence of the LORD, we automatically bow down at His Feet, with head to the ground. It is the LORD who will graciously ask us to rise up and not to fear Him.

Yes, the LORD is our friend, and beloved, and we can draw close to Him, and look up to Him, face to Face without fear of death or rebuke, because The LORD has accepted us as His own, all because of Jesus Christ, who is our righteousness.

We give all the glory, praise and worship unto God, our Father, for He is worthy of praise, honor and glory, and we echo the angels in Heaven, who will declare the glory of the LORD, all over the world.

God, our Father is deserving of all praise and worship. When we arrive in Heaven, we will be praising God with the angels, all day and there will be no night.

We humble ourselves before the Living God and give Him all the Glory, all the Honor, and all the Praise.

Haughty men or women of the world, bursting with pride or ego seek their personal honor, glory and praise, either due or not necessarily due to them, and continue to boost their personal ego, not acknowledging that all their success comes from God.

It is the very reason that the infamous angel fell from grace, from heaven for wanting to be highly honored.

Give worship and praise to our Heavenly Father for He alone is worthy of praise and worship. In return, our Father is pleased and blesses us.

In whatever situation or dilemma, we may be in, when we praise and worship God, with thanksgiving, the atmosphere changes, and victory over the air takes place, and success follows.

Praise and worship conquer the unseen realm, and the angels of God are released to do God's work among the peoples, especially for you, your family and your workplace.

Love our Father with all our heart, all our mind, all our soul and all our strength and worship Him, head to the ground, before the Throne of Grace at His feet.

[The opposite of love is hate. It is true that no one who knows the Father will hate Him.

Yet, the Word says that we can only either love God or Mammon, not both. And if one loves one, one will hate the other. It does seem that the scale of 'Love' is a skewed one. We have to choose one or the other. If we choose God, our Father, then we have to hate money and riches.

It must be like marriage. You agree to marry, and your eyes, heart, mind and soul has to be for your spouse and your spouse only. On a weekday, can you go around kissing, hugging, caressing other women or men. Or can you engage in sexual talk or texting with others, even though no indecent act is done.

Love for God our Father means you have one choice or one pick, and that one pick has to be God, our Father.

Interestingly, although it seems to be that you now `hate' all others, as it is implied, - in actual fact, when you love our Father, you will love all that our Father loves, which is all of creation.

The opposite of worship is blasphemy, apart from the lack of worship or bowing down to our Father.

This author has deliberately, perhaps Holy Spirit guided, put this as the last not because it is of the least importance but in reflection of what our Father says, "that He can raise stones to worship Him." This suggests that our Father is more pleased when we obey Him and do His work, rather than be a lazy son, who wakes up from his sloth to worship Him, before going back to booze and sin.

An evil example of such sons were the sons of a certain priest who were involved with fornication right in the temple doors, provoking God's anger.

Blasphemy can be in so many forms, not necessarily identical to another faith, where the law of the land includes possible frivolous remarks as such.

Taking our Father's Name in vain would be 'blasphemy'. In reality, the Name of our Father and His Son Jesus, has suffered much by many blasphemous acts and words.

For those who do not know our Father, we plead mercy and grace. It is for those who know our Father, that we must warn that their continued deeds and words can cause their fall from grace, and many such Christian leaders have fallen.]

TWELVE   Humility & Meekness

Humility and meekness go together as two sides of a gem, a beautiful one, that is radiant before God and men.

Placed last here in a list of twelve attributes or expectations of our Father of a son or daughter, it stands out high as a very important attribute, one of true humility and meekness.

The realization and eventual empowerment through the attainment of sonship should be accompanied with humility and meekness, for the position of sonship literally is so high and anointed that the son or daughter can misuse or abuse his or her position, if this exaltation does not come with humility and meekness. Our Father knows that, for when He gave all authority and power to the Son, Jesus, He knew it comes with great responsibility, with humility and meekness, as the Lord went humbly to the Cross, in all meekness for the salvation of mankind.

He could have ordered a legion of angels to deliver Him from the grasp and authority of mere men, but did not, for He came to fulfill the will of our Father.

We too, me and you too, for we are here to fulfill the will of
Father God, and not for our own delight or pleasure.

The Bible tells of Moses, one of the greatest of all prophets,
or men who lived on the face of the earth, one whom God our
Father says that He speaks Face to face.

The Bible describes Moses as the most humble or meekest
among all men on earth.

Numbers 12:3, "Now, the man Moses was very humble,
more than all men who were on the face of the earth."

Let us pause here to understand the position of Moses. In
modern day, he would still be considered as a very powerful
person, whether in the eyes of men, in the area of religion
and faith, and also in the eyes of God.

His deeds were well known among the people of that time.
He was firstly raised as a prince in the house of Pharaoh.
That alone, places him very high in the secular and royal
sense, being only a step or two from the throne or Pharaoh, or
equivalent to that of a governor or of a powerful king or
emperor.

He was also the only one who could meet the LORD GOD,
our Father, face to FACE. And, he could speak to God, the
LORD, one to ONE, and the LORD would respond to his
plea and request.

His prayer was not a nebulous, uncertainty, but a direct
talking and meeting with God, and God considered Moses as
His highly favored prophet, messenger and even friend.

When Moses requested to see God, God consented and arranged a meeting, with Moses standing behind a rock and having a glimpse of God's Glory as God passed by.

In one awesome meeting, when God, the LORD was going to present a second set of tablets bearing the 'Ten Commandments', Hand written by God directly to Moses alone on Mount Sinai, no man or animal were to be present on the mountain.

The LORD descended early that morning in a cloud and stood with Moses, proclaiming His Name – the name of the LORD.

Exodus 34:6,7 "And the LORD passed before him and proclaimed, 'The LORD, the LORD God, merciful and gracious, longsuffering, and abounding in goodness and truth, keeping mercy for thousands, forgiving iniquity and transgression and sin, by no means clearing the guilty, visiting the iniquity of the fathers upon the children, and the children's children to the third and fourth generation."

The next verse describes Moses as bowing his head towards the earth and worshipping God.

Moses immediately interceded to God for the sake of the people, with a passionate plea recorded in verse 9:

"If now I have found grace in Your sight, O Lord, let my Lord, I pray go among us, even though we are a stiff-nicked people; and pardon our iniquity and our sin, and take us as Your inheritance."

The LORD responded positively to Moses plea to bless the people. Moses repeated this more than once when going through the struggles of the people in the directs. In Numbers 14:18, the very same stiff-necked people angered the LORD

and He was about to destroy them, but through the grace of
God, and the divine intervention of Moses, the destruction
was called off.

Such is his influence and power, - a direct access to Almighty
God, the LORD, that in present day world, it would make
Moses the most powerful man on earth, and who have ever
lived on earth.

Yet, Moses is described as being the most humble or meek
among all men

As much power and authority is vested in the believer, the
Christian, humility and meekness is so vital, because in its
absence, with pride and arrogance seeping in, this authority
and power can be abused or misused, to the detriment of the
Kingdom of God. For that reason, we need to humble
ourselves before the LORD, for in due time, we will be
exalted, when it is safe for us to be so empowered and
powerful.

The Scriptures are clear, that the "meek shall inherit the
earth", not the rich or the powerful.

Psalm 37:11, "But the meek shall inherit the earth, and shall
delight themselves in the abundance of peace."

Jesus Himself declared with authority as the Son of God, in
Matthew 5:5, "Blessed are the meek, for they shall inherit the
earth."

God our Father desires us to be humble and meek, for He has
already prepared the whole earth for you and I, to hand it to
us. Why so? Because, we would have passed the supreme test
– one of meekness and humility!

For God, our Father hates the proud, and would take all away from the proud and give it to the humble and meek..

Why should any among us worry, clamor or rush for honor, glory or position, for God will exalt us and raise us up, if we are humble and meek. Remember, that is the very reason, Jesus emphasized that the "first will be last and the last first." God's order and formula is totally different from that of the world. For you and I are in the world but not of the world.

1 Peter 5:6 assures us, "Therefore, humble yourselves under the Mighty Hand of God, that He may exalt you in due time."

The verse before that urges the younger people to submit themselves to the elders, and be submissive (meek and humble) to one another, and 'be clothed with humility.'

We are reminded that "God resists the proud, but gives grace to the humble." This is recorded in the preceding verse.

God, our Father really hates the proud and haughty.

Proverbs 6:16-19 says, "These six things, the LORD hates, yes, seven are an abomination to Him: a proud look, a lying tongue, hands that shed innocent blood, a heart that devises wicked plans, feet that are swift in running to evil, a false witness who speaks lies, and one who sows discord among brethren."

The Bible talks of evil in these last days in 2 Timothy 3:1-5, "For men will be lovers of themselves, lovers of money, boasters, proud, blasphemers, disobedience to parents, unthankful and unholy, unloving, unforgiving, slanderers, without self-control, brutal, despisers of good, traitors, headstrong, haughty, lovers of pleasure, rather than of God, having a form of godliness, but denying its power.."

The tendency of the proud is to declare that 'one is great', 'one is self-sufficient or self-sustainable' or declaring all one's achievement is through one's own efforts, or even be so bold as to equate one as being like 'God'.

In reality, there is no such thing as 'man can do everything by man's own strength and might and ability!'

Man, or mankind is great and intelligent and powerful, only on the virtue that God has empowered man to 'multiply, fill the earth and subdue it', all by God-given strength and power.

It is true that man's intelligence has allowed man to breakdown and understand the some of the forces of nature, and the great resources of the earth, for the first man had vegetation and the accompaniment of the things of nature, apart from the fishes of the sea, the birds of the air and the creatures on earth.

From all that, we now have supersonic jets, towering skyscrapers and awesome towers, and great devices like the smartphone and the internet, apart from weapons of mass destruction – all made possible through the mind of man.

But man remains a mortal. The moment he prides himself that he will get richer and richer, and build a bigger and bigger barn for his business, without acknowledging God humbly, he may receive a note from the Maker, saying, "Time's up!" I am taking you home tonight. Lease is up!

Jesus Himself told of a man who intended to build a greater barn in Luke 12:18-20, "Fool, this night your soul will be required of you."
Again, in Acts 12:22-23, we read of King Herod who urged the people to praise him by saying, "the voice of a god and

not of man", when an angel of the LORD struck him dead, and his body was immediately full of maggots.

The Bible says that he did not give Glory to God.

So, humility and meekness acknowledges that it is God that has elevated us to be a son or daughter and we should not be proud, but must be humble and meek before men, even though we are placed in position higher.

Jesus also told the story of one who wishes to be recognized and to be seated in front, in contrast to one who is humble and chooses to be seated behind, and is then invited to the front.

How then can we be more humble and meek? By recognizing that whatever we have achieved, whatever position we are in, whatever riches we have, we have arrived at our destination because of God, not because of our own might and strength, for that is the truth. That it is because of God, that we are alive, and that we have been elevated.

So, why should we boast or be proud, for all that we have achieved is through God's grace.

The benefit of humility and meekness is obvious; it is the secret or passport to the full inheritance of the earth – the whole earth.

[The opposite of humility is pride, and pride comes before the fall, and the prince of the earth is the best example of such a one. Let us emulate the Lord, who humbled Himself and went to the Cross, not the other one.]

SUMMARY   The Extra Mile

The rich man came to Jesus and said that he had done everything, and he enquired what else he should do?

Matthew 19:20-21 relates this incidence, "The young man said to Him, 'All these things I have kept from my youth What do I still lack?'

Jesus said to him, 'If you want to be perfect, go, sell what you have and give to the poor, and you will have treasure in heaven; and come, follow Me."

The rich man could not take this teaching, and he went away sorrowful, for he had great possessions.

Then there is the often-quoted teaching of going the extra mile and offering the other cheek.

These are two seemingly extreme teachings that make the ordinary Christian shudder.

In Matthew 5:39-41, Jesus said, "But I tell you not to resist an evil person. But whoever slaps you on the right cheek, turn the other to him also."
"If anyone wants to sue you and take away your tunic, let him have your cloak also."
"And whoever compels you to go one mile, go with him two."

The attribute that perhaps sums up this last teaching of Jesus is one of 'total surrender' to the Lord, for when we place Him first, and we become of no consequence or importance, then pride, self-importance and ego will give way to meekness, humility and a truly servanthood, where the

Master comes first always, and to do His will becomes of the utmost importance.

The well-known Chinese author Watchman Nee's motto was, "I want everything for my Lord, and nothing for myself."

How meek and humble are we? How much do we do for ourselves, think of ourselves, and how important is the Lord in comparison to me, myself, mine and "I"?

It is perhaps easier at the end of one's life to totally surrender at His Feet, and be at His Majesty's Service, but if you have the calling and the grace to do so earlier in life, you may have found the higher and better calling.

When you totally surrender to our Lord, then all attributes from one to twelve become automatically and naturally a part of you and in you.

But even before then, you can arise and do something. What then should we do now? What is the author's target in writing this booklet?

Obviously, it is to raise generations of good sons and daughters, this author included. For certainty, every believer will endeavor to be a good son or daughter.

Our Father so desires that we are not just only His, as we already are, but to be a good son and a good daughter. And it will be for our own good, if we walk the path and receive the exalted position of sonship (daughters too).

For we are reminded again and again, that all things come from our Father through His Son, and without Him, there was nothing made, that was made.

We are also reminded, that apart from Jesus, we can do nothing, but with God, all things are possible. We are in fact the branch, and we must if not need to be attached to the Vine, which is our Master and Lord.

It is so natural and so obvious, if we are scuba diving, we will not cut off our oxygen tubing that is connected to the oxygen tank, which is Jesus. Likewise, the astronaut on a walk outside the spacecraft would be suicidal if he went out without his life support and tubing.

The LORD GOD knows you by name. He is a gentleman, and has been waiting for you for years and years.

Father has been awaiting your call, for you to call Him Father; you have a direct line to call to Him, from your heart, mind and soul to Father's Heart.

Acknowledge Father, as your God and LORD God, and call Him today. More than that, acknowledge that He is the Majesty, and that He is Awesome in might and power. Declare Him your Master, as you surrender at His Feet.

As you thank and appreciate Father for all that He has done for you, especially saving you and setting you free, - free from captivity, free from bondage, free from fears, free from addictions, free from oppression, free from the enemy, you will renew your relationship with Father, and be renewed and refreshed in strength and vitality, even in youthfulness. You will spread out your wings and rise and fly high as an eagle. The truth has set you free.

As you begin to walk in your obedience, being loyal and faithful to the LORD, living a life pleasing to Father God, being a parent yourself, and a good steward to those under your authority, your prayers and worship reach out to Father, and you have arrived at the threshold of a new beginning.

Father will look you up, and call you for His work and ministry. You will be "sent", whether near or far, for the work that awaits you!

You are already as a royal priest, an ambassador, as a spokesperson. All you need to do is to claim it, receive it, and like a royal garment, put it on and embark on your journey and mission. You do not necessarily need a theological training, as Father will equip you, and your local church and elders assists this sending off with prayer and anointing with oil.

One error or confusion or even wrong teaching by the churches is to declare the 'new believer' being not ready – not ready for baptism in water, not ready for sharing the gospel, not ready to be sent out, even after months and years warming the pulpit. Who then is ready, and who then can be 'sent'?

This author has seen and witness a young believer, in the form of a personal grandniece, barely 10 or 11 years of age, having just accepted Jesus as Savior together with the parents, being able to minister effectively in the spiritual realm, within just 24 hours as a new believer.

In a very short declaration that "Jesus is Lord", she was able to release the power of the ministering and warring angels, and the 'demonic disturbances' that have been manifesting in their home for seven years just fled, in that short little prayer.

Many who believe can be baptized in water immediately, as in the case of the Ethiopian eunuch, and many in fact even receive baptism of the Holy Spirit, simultaneously when they receive Jesus.

A week-old Christian, even a day-old Christian can lead people to Jesus. Do not keep waiting, or to say it correctly, "Do not keep the Lord Jesus waiting for you."

You are ready, equipped and empowered once born again in the Spirit of Christ; you are immediately transferred as a pauper in darkness, to become a rich prince, priest and prophet in God's Holy Presence.

All you need to say is, "I believe in Jesus, that He is the Son of God and Savior of the World." No matter what the others around you may say, whether in rebuke, persecution, or ridicule, just reply that as far as you are concerned, "Jesus is Lord" and you are pleased that you can declare so.

Tell them that if ever they are in need or trouble, just declare that "Jesus is Lord", and it will be a breakthrough for them, when they do so sincerely.

The Lord Jesus' last command was to "Go out into the world, from your `hometown', your `neighborhood" and the rest of the world, making disciples of all men!"

You need not be perfect to be a truly 'good son.' Only God is good, as Jesus said, when one called him 'Good Teacher'. Our goodness is in Him, and our strength and ability are in the Lord. All we need to do is to abide in Jesus and He will be our strength, for He will never fail us nor forsake us, and Jesus is always on our right-hand side. (Psalm 16.8)

The key then, is always to follow the LORD.

Seek Him always, not rarely, sometimes, or when you are in trouble or need. When you call upon our Father daily, and you draw close to Him affectionately, and you dwell lovingly in His Presence, you will find yourself doing wonders and miracles.

Following God is not a mindless chanting while reading the newspapers, or reciting prayers by heart, but making an eye to Eye, mind to Mind, heart to Heart contact with the Almighty.

Dedicating a different day of the week to a different attribute, or focusing each month of the year on each attribute, one by one, you will go higher and higher, deeper and deeper, and further and further in your friendship and relationship with Father God.

He will call you and speak to you.

But long before He does, you can declare to the LORD, - "LORD, here I am, surrendered at Your Feet, ready to serve You."

It's as simple as that.

The good son and good daughter have been born today. like our Savior Jesus was and is yesterday, today and tomorrow.

Jesus does what the Father does, and He came down, because our Father sent Him. Jesus did what He saw our Father did, and Jesus does nothing apart from what He saw our Father does. (John 3:16,17 & John 5.19)

So, too for us, when we were young and we enjoyed following our dad or mum around, and dad and mum would call upon us to assist him or her. "Bring me the hammer, and we would run. Or mum would say, pass me the pepper and we would gladly do so." We would be so pleased at the end of the day, when Papa would say, "Son, we did it together. We build this fence together. Now our sheep is safe from the wolves." Or mum would say, "Girl, we cooked this meal together. You can tell Papa that you and Mummy cooked this dish called "Mama's Special Stew". Papa will ask why it is special and you can tell him that it is because you were part of the cooking process."

Yes, let us do what Jesus did – go out and preach the Good News, heal the sick and raise the dead, and as Jesus said, we will do greater things than He did.

John 14.12 will be fulfilled in your life, when you agree to follow His call and then go out wherever He sends you and I! You will no longer live your life as a fisherman who has caught not a single fish in his or her life. But for Christ and in Christ, you will indeed be a fisher of men.

Pray like this:

"LORD, let me be a good son, to follow in your footsteps and to go, as you have sent me. I pray in Jesus Name."

Amen.

REVELATION

The Son of God Revealed

This title on "The Good Son" will be incomplete without a discourse about "The Good Son", the one and only truly good son – "The Son of God" Himself.

We can never understand or appreciate the magnitude of this revelation unless we look at the history of mankind from the very beginning at least, if not to the end.

Let us take it to the very beginning. Adam and Eve being the first prototype had the singular privilege of face to Face meetings with the LORD, the Maker of all things.

Adam knew that God was God. This may be an assumption but it is almost certainly so, as the Book of Genesis so plainly states.

God being the Maker saw and observed His creation, and said, "It was good." We read in Psalms 104 how the fishes of the sea wait for God for food, and how the young lion roar after their prey and seek their food from God, mighty as the lions are, and free as the fishes are in roaming the seas.

They have kept their knowledge of the Maker until this day.

So, Adam and Eve knew the LORD, and spoke face to Face from day one, till they fell in sin, resulting in a gulf of silence and communications, until men began to call upon the Name of the LORD.

Somehow, since that time, as man continues to seek after God, and hear from God from the voices of the prophets and seers, there was and still is some sort of 'gulf' or barrier between God and man.

But deep inside the soul of man was the hunger waiting for God to literally come down on to earth again, as the Messiah as predicted in the Old Testament.

In Micah 5:2, we read, "But you, Bethlehem Ephrathah, you are little among the thousands of Judah, yet out of you shall come forth to Me, the One to be Ruler in Israel, Whose goings forth are from of old, from everlasting."

So, the people of Israel have been waiting for thousands of
years, for a great king, a great prophet, a "Son of God" in fact
to come.

And when this Son comes, He will truly stand out and
transform the world literally, an awesome event for mankind,
a breakthrough of breakthrough.

It is a much-awaited event, for the scholars, for the prophets,
for the teachers, for all of Israel who know that The LORD is
God, and the God of Abraham, the God of Isaac, the God of
Jacob is the Creator and God of the whole earth.
Who is He, where is He, when will He come, how will he
come, and in what way will He come, and in what way will
He show Himself or manifest? All these were not clearly
spelt out or defined, so much so that until today, two major
religions in the world are still waiting for the majestic arrival
of the King of kings, whether they refer to Him as Messiah or
Mahdi.

As Christians, we believe that the Messiah has already come,
and has dwelt with us, and shown His Glory to His people,
and continues to live in us.

What perhaps may have confused the learned and wise men
of old was the interpretation of what would happen with His
Coming, especially that it is His Second Coming that refers
to judgment, and the End itself.

We believe that the first coming was one of grace and love,
as a baby, born of a virgin mother, unblemished and growing
up to be the manifest presence of God.

He did not remain a baby, hut was soon revealed at age 33
years, when God send John the Baptist ahead of Jesus, to
perform the ritual of baptism, as a sign of repentance before
God Almighty. Many believed and lined up obediently to be

baptized in the River Jordan, repenting of their sins, as they prepared their hearts to receive the Savior of the world.

Then, we now know that He has already come, and there is actually a Second Coming, when Jesus will return as a Mighty King, a Ruler over Israel, the season and times that the prophets have referred to and the people of Israel, now the world are waiting for.

Let us now look at the evidence or the revelation of the Son of God.

Firstly, a son is a son, and a son who is an heir is the rightful son, empowered to take over the Father, or given as much authority to do so, to rule as the Father.

Thus, the Son of God is the Son of God and is equal to God. That is how awesome and powerful it is, when we come to the full realization as to who Jesus is.

The first evidence must be the witnesses.

Mary, the Blessed Mother of Jesus must surely stand out as the sole and most prominent witness and testimony to Jesus for she was the Immaculate Conception, and was visited by angel Gabriel himself before she was conceived by the Holy Spirit or Spirit of God.

Imagine this: if the Queen of the United Kingdom or the President of America were to come and visit your country, and was scheduled to stay in a particular suite of a particular hotel. It would take months of preparation to identify the particular room and to sanctify and seal it as the Royal or Presidential Room, and keep it immaculate for the Queen or President to arrive and use it.

So too, with the Blessed Mother of Jesus, who was hand picked by God, and sanctified, cleansed and made immaculate to prepare for the arrival of the King of kings, and the Lord of lords, who would spend a precious nine months in her womb, and grew up as an infant and toddler for some years, before the child becomes a man – the Son of Man.

Mary heard from angel Gabriel, and Mary immediately received a touch from God, and Joseph too was visited in a dream, and Joseph immediately did not touch Mary for she had now a great mission before her, as she was to conceive and her child would be called Immanuel or Jesus, for He would save His people from sin.

"The Holy Spirit will come upon you, and the power of the Highest will overshadow you, therefore, also, that Holy One who is to be born will be called the Son of God." Luke 1:35.

These were the words that the angel spoke to Mary, the blessed mother of Jesus.

So, Blessed Mother Mary had infant Jesus in her womb for nine months and she knew that she was carrying the 'Son of God.'

At the right time, she visited Elizabeth her cousin, who also had a divine conception, a baby anointed by God to be the messenger and prophet who would prepare the way for Jesus, the Son of God. Baby John (the Baptist) leaped up with joy in the womb of mother Elizabeth, when he sensed the Presence of the Almighty Son of God.

Then, at Bethlehem, at the birth of Jesus, Mary (who already knew without the slightest doubt that Jesus, her Son by that angels singing had directed them to visited and worship the Savior, a baby born to save mankind.

It was an angel of the LORD that stood before them, and the glory of the LORD shone around them, bringing great fear among them, signifying God's awesome Presence. Yet the Bible says that the angel assured them and declared, "Behold, I bring you good tidings of great joy which will be to all people. For there is born to you this day in the city of David a Savior, who is Christ the Lord. And this will the sign to you. You will find a Bab wrapped in swaddling cloth, lying in a manger." Luke 2:10-13.

This was followed by an awesome display literally of a multitude (a large number) of heavenly host (of angels) praising God and saying:

"Glory to God in the Highest, and on earth peace, goodwill toward men!" Luke 2:14

It was such an awesome sight, experience and feeling that the shepherds with one heart decided to go to Bethlehem, with or without their flock, to see "this thing that has come to pass, which the LORD has made known to us."

The Bible says in Luke 2:16-19:

"And they came with haste and found Mary and Joseph, and the Babe (spelt with capital) lying in a manger. Now when they had seen Him, they made widely known the saying which was told them concerning this Child. And those who heard it marveled at those things, which were told them by the shepherds.
But Mary kept all these things and pondered them in her heart."

Soon after, following Jewish custom, the Child, Baby Jesus was circumcised on the 8th day.

Luke 2:21 "His name was called JESUS, the name given by the angel before He was conceived in the womb."

So, after the days of purification as in the law of Moses, for Blessed Mary, the mother of Jesus, Jesus as brought to Jerusalem to be presented to the LORD.

On arrival in the temple in Jerusalem, a prophet named Simeon, a devout man and just one, who had been waiting for the Messiah or Consolation of Israel, was moved by the Holy Spirit. It was revealed to him by the Holy Spirit that he would not die before seeing 'The LORD's Child' or the 'Son of God', and to do for Jesus according to the custom of the law.

He took JESUS up in his arms, and blessed God and said:

"LORD, now You are letting Your servant depart in peace. According to Your Word; For my eyes have seen Your Salvation, which You have prepared before the face of all peoples, a light to bring revelation to the Gentiles, and the Glory of Your people Israel." Lue 2:31,32.

All these things said was heard by Joseph and His mother Mary, and they marveled at those things which were spoken of Jesus.

Simeon went on to bless them, and prophesied to Mary, "Behold, this Child is destined for the fall and rising of many in Israel, and for a sign which will be spoken against (yes, a sword will pierce through your own soul also), that the thoughts of man hearts may be revealed."

At the same time, there was a prophetess Anna, the daughter of Phanuel, of the tribe of Asher, who was elderly who served God, day and night in prayers and fasting, giving thanks to the LORD, and spoke of Jesus that all will look to Him for redemption.

Not long after, the three wise men from the East came and brought His Majesty, baby Jesus gifts of myrrh, gold and frankincense as they too worship the King of kings, who had just been born.

In obedience to the angel, Joseph and Mary fled with infant Jesus to Egypt to stay there to be safe from King Herod who had heard that a king was born. Thinking that this was a physical king who would one day threaten his throne, he had sought out to kill all male babies under a certain age, in an attempt to eliminate such a child born during that season.

There were no immigration checkpoints then, and hence the king's plan failed as Jesus had already escaped.

Joseph and the mother of Jesus continued to witness as JESUS grew and became strong in spirit, filled with wisdom, and the grace of God was upon Him.

Mary's further revelation that Jesus, her Son was the Messiah came when by the young age of twelve, as they went to Jerusalem for the Feast of the Passover, Jesus stayed behind for three days, talking to the teachers discussing with them the things of God.

They were all "astonished and amazed at His understanding and answers."

When finally found by parents, Joseph and Mary and questioned why he was missing, Jesus declared that He was in "doing His Father's business", clearly stating that He was the Son of God, at that young age of twelve.

As we fast forward, the time finally arrives at River Jordan. This is the work and ministry of John the Baptist, who was already a recognized prophet of God. He had probably for many years declaring that the Messiah was coming, and everyone needed to prepare their hearts, beginning with serious genuine repentance, followed by the process of water baptism by full immersion in the River Jordan.

The Bible says that all the people in the vicinity – all came. All means all, i.e. not even one soul was left out, except the Pharisees and the Sadducees, who refrained and were even reprimanded for their hardness of heart. They had not yet repented.

While Blessed Mother Mary was and is the best testimony and witness that Jesus is the Son of God, hers was personal experience and a private one, while John the Baptist was a public figure and his evidence is seen by everyone.

John stopped at whatever he was doing, while baptizing someone, when he stopped, stunned, gazing in the direct of Jesus and stated clearly:

"This is the Lamb of God, who takes away the sin of the people."

Already, everyone who came was baptized in the water by emersion, it was John the Baptist who told them that he was nothing compared to the One whose sandals he was unworthy to tie. In fact, if not for the order given to him but the angel of God, he would have declined that esteemed role to baptize the Son of God himself.

Those present also would have heard as the Voice of God from heavens spoke out loud, as Jesus was baptized by John the Baptist and on rising up from the waters, the Holy Spirit descended like a dove on Jesus and God spoke.

Matthew 3:16,17, "When He had been baptized, Jesus came up immediately from the water; and behold, the heavens were opened to Him and He saw the Spirit of God descending like a dove and alighting upon Him.
And suddenly a voice came from heaven, saying, **"This is My beloved Son, in whom I am well pleased."**

This is the testimony from God the Father Himself that Jesus is the Son of God.

At Cana, just before Jesus began His ministry, the mother of Jesus was at a family wedding and the host ran out of wine and was helpless. Mary, the Blessed mother of Jesus asked the host to tell Jesus. Jesus had not yet begun the ministry, yet He obliged and the first miracle of water turning to the best wine was performed for His mother's sake.

Jesus began His ministry by calling disciples, who followed Him. He exhibited His awesome authority by a simple call, "Come, follow Me." One by one would drop whatever they are doing to follow Jesus. They knew Him from the very start as a teacher and a prophet.

Some were very quick to believe, possibly being guided by the Spirit of God. Philip declared to Nathanael and said. "We have found Hm of whom Moses in the law, and also the prophets wrote – Jesus of Nazareth, the son of Joseph."

Nathanael was perhaps the first to know, believe and declare it, almost at the first encounter, "Rabbi, You are the Son of God! You are the King of Israel." John 1:49

Peter came to the awesome realization when Jesus stopped the storm with a word, "You are the Christ, the Son of the living God." Matthew 16:16

Martha, who was very close to Jesus also declared, "Yes, Lord, I believe that You are the Christ, the Son of God, who is to come into the world."

She said this just before her brother Lazarus was resurrected from the dead, and just after Jesus had declared that "I am the Resurrection and the Life."

Of course, the demons also testified when they cried out, "What have we to do with You, Jesus, You Son of God?" before they entered the herd of swine and drowned in the waters. Matthew 8:29.

We will not use the testimony of the liar who quoted it three times and said, "if You are the Son of God" in the attempt to tempt Jesus.

After the crucifixion, as Jesus laid down His life, and there was darkness and earthquakes shook the earth, the centurion and those around Jesus at the cross realized and said, "Truly, this was the Son of God!" Matthew 27:54

Finally, these are the testimonies from the Bible, the Word of God itself, and the testimonies from the Son of God Himself.

The Good Son, the Son of God was there from the beginning and remains with us till the very end.

He was there in the beginning of Creation with the Father, when it is written: "In the beginning, God created the heavens and the earth." The passages in Genesis continue with the pronoun "We".

The Gospel of John affirms it, in Chapter One, verse 1 to 3.

"In the beginning was the Word and the Word was with God and the Word was God." Word here refers to Jesus.

Verse three of the same Gospel speaks very powerfully that "All things were made through Hm, and without Him nothing was made that was made."

Everything on earth that we see, living and dead, even the earth itself was made by God, through the Son, both being Co-Creators with the Spirit of God.

During the short but powerful ministry of Jesus as He appeared and walked on planet earth, Jesus Himself declared Who He was. Unlike, other teachers and prophets and founders of other faiths and religions, he did more than just point to the correct path and teach what was right and what was wrong.

Jesus pointed to Himself to say "Who am I."

"I am the Way, the Truth and the Life. No one comes to the Father except through Me." John 14:6

"I am the true vine, and My Father the vinedresser." John 15:1

"I am in the Father and the Father in Me." John 14:10,11

"I and My Father are one." John 10:30

"All things that the Father has are Mine." John 16:15

"All authority has been given to Me in heaven and on earth." Matthew 28:18

"Because I go to My Father and you see Me no more;" John 16:10

All these verses confirm that Jesus is the Son of God, and the last verse in Matthew powerfully asserts that full trust and empowering is now with the Son, the Son of God, who is the Boss, the King of kings and the LORD of lords.

You and I may ask, "So what?"

So that we know who is the Boss and who to go to for help!

For the Scriptures say, "For without Me (Jesus), you can do nothing." John 15.5

Yet, with God all things are possible. Matthew 19:26

And this is the connection or cable towards power:

"And whatever you ask in My name, that I will do that the Father may be glorified in the Son. If you ask anything in My name, I will do it." John 14:13,14

This is the "Son of God" revealed and His Name is Jesus.

The amazing and awesome revelation is that this Savior, this Son of God, is now our friend, for Jesus Himself calls us His friend, and for sure, everyone wants an all-powerful, Omnipotent Friend like Jesus.

John 15:15, "No longer do I call you servants… but I have called you friends, for all things that I heard from My Father I have made known to you."

This is the Word of God revealed for us, that God sent His Son into the World to be our Savior and Friend, so that we can have a good and happy life in Him, an abundant life.

EPILOGUE   This son

How do I as the author consider myself as a 'son'?

As a son to my biological parents, I would rate myself poorly, a 'C" at the best, in a scale from A to F, where F is a bad fail ranging upwards to an A for excellent.

As, this book is focused on our Heavenly Father, I would say that there are probably only two grades, i.e. a pass and a fail. I believe that I made the grade the moment I called upon the Name of the LORD, when I found my LORD, through His Son and Savior Jesus.

My journey towards being a 'son' began when I decided to search for God Almighty at my mature age of 30 years, then already a doctor.

I grew up in a traditional Chinese family, being the third generation from a Chinese migrant to Malaya, from Swatow, China. We practiced a combination of Taoism, with Buddhism, and also prayed to several deities. Both Taoism and Confucianism emphasized the importance of being a filial son.

At age 30 years, then a young doctor, I began to question my real faith, and decided that I was in fact a 'Free thinker', or one with no clear beliefs.

All that changed when I decided to seriously search for the living God. Pondering on what were the options available e.g. go on a solo extended meditation trip, seek and follow a spiritual teacher or guru, or seriously study the scriptures. I opted for the last, - to seriously study the scriptures. At that time, I was prepared to read various Holy Books, whether Buddhist texts, teachings of Confucius, the Bhagavad Gita, Koran, Holy Books of Sikhism, or the Bible, before coming to a conclusion or decision.

I chose the Bible and began a serious self-study and reading beginning from the first book in Genesis. It was a long and winding road, as I trudged along in my daily reading, day after day searching for the Living God.

On looking back, it was a search for our Heavenly Father.

The stories and teachings from the Old Testament were so rich and fascinating, that I began to have a deeper understanding of man's faltering relationship with God, then the God of the Bible.

At the end of five months, I had completed the Old Testament, and two major events had already taken place or was happening in my life. The first was the birth of my first child Grace, who was born in July of that year, 1981. The next major event was my first travel abroad to the United Kingdom for my postgraduate studies and examination.

It was during this far away experience many thousand miles away, long before the mobile phone and e-mail or internet communication came into existence, that I was intensely searching and reading into the New Testament. My five months search through thorough reading of the Old Testament had literally prepared by heart for the next encounter – the arrival of the Messiah Himself.

In literally two to three weeks, I had 'marched' from the Gospel of Matthew to the Book of Corinthians, while my heart raced from being a spiritual 'orphan' into the potential adoption as a `son' of the Most High God.

The full story is related in my e-book "How I Became a Christian".

Basically, I believed in Jesus, as Messiah and Son of God, as early as my readings in Matthew's Gospel, but it was around the readings into the Book of Corinthians, that I surrendered my life to the Father, and received my son-ship, not born by blood or water but by the Spirit of God.

What then, or what now, since I am already a `son' of our Heavenly Father? Am I a 'good son'? I am reminded by our Lord Jesus, that "only God is good!".

I therefore continue to walk the path on earth, as best as I can, knowing that each man or woman's path and walk is different, guided by His Divine

Whatever we do, we should do it unto the LORD, and do it with a sincere heart, giving our best, with all our might, our strength, our mind and our soul.

In so doing, we do well, and need not worry or fear as to how well we did it, as long as we do so, unto the LORD, our Heavenly Father.

THE AUTHOR

Dr Timothy Sng is a medical doctor and neurologist by profession. A born-again believer for nearly four decades, his passion is to seek out the 'lost sons and daughters' for the Kingdom of God. His personal mission is to seek our Father in Heaven daily to be a faithful servant and son.

Other mini e-books on Amazon include 'How I Became a Christian', 'Why I am a Christian', 'The Good & Precious Wife'. 'Once Saved Forever Safe', 'God is No Delusion', 'The First Christmas', 'J2C Alert', 'Words Alive', 'The Gospel in 30 Minutes', 'The Ten Minute Gospel John 3:16', 'The Power of One Verse Exodus 34:6', 'The Instant Gospel', and 'The Power of One Verse Deuteronomy 4:39', 'The Ten Minute Gospel John3:17', 'Googling for God', and 'The Power of One Verse Exodus 23:25'.

Email: drtimothysng@gmail.com
www.timsng.blogspot.com